REIGNITING the AMERICAN DREAM

A Bold Blueprint for Confronting Leftist Extremism and Revitalizing Democracy

Robert Dobbs

CONTENTS

Introduction

There is a complicated and controversial discourse around socialism and its implications for the future of the United States of America. This discourse frequently divides public opinion and provokes discussion among academics. In its most fundamental form, socialism may be understood as an economic and political philosophy that advocates for the ownership and administration of the means of production and distribution of products by a collective or governmental entity. This philosophy tries to solve concerns of economic inequality and social injustice by advocating for the distribution of wealth, the establishment of social welfare programs, and the abolition of class hierarchies. On the other hand, socialism is not a singular ideology; rather, it covers a wide range of distinct ideas, ranging from democratic socialism to more extreme variants, such as Marxism.

A criticism of capitalism that is centered on the idea of class struggle is presented by Marxism, which is a form of socialism that was created in the 19th century by Karl Marx and Friedrich Engels. It is the contention of Marxists that capitalism fundamentally exploits the working class, also known as the proletariat, for the advantage of the owning class, also known as the bourgeoisie, which results in social and economic inequality. They call for the revolutionary destruction of capitalism systems in order to initiate the establishment of a society without classes in which resources and power are divided in an equitable manner. Marxists sometimes highlight the necessity for drastic change, sometimes by revolutionary methods, in contrast to democratic socialists, who aim to accomplish their goals through progressive reform within existing political structures. Marxists may also aspire to achieve their goals through revolutionary means.

It is important to investigate the possible influence that socialism, and Marxism in particular, might have on the future of the United States of America for a number of reasons. First and foremost, it makes it possible to conduct an in-depth analysis of the present economic and social difficulties that the United States of America is facing, such as the disparity in income, the accessibility of healthcare, and the rights of workers. In the second place, it offers a perspective that may be utilized to contemplate alternative models of economic organization and governance that have the potential to address these challenges. Thirdly, the dispute between socialism and capitalism focuses on basic values and concepts, such as freedom, equality, and the role that the government plays in the lives of individuals.

On top of that, the conversation is quite current. There has been a resurgence of interest in socialist ideals among some elements of the American people, particularly among younger generations, in recent years. This interest has been particularly prevalent among younger generations. This transition is a reflection of rising worries about the viability of existing economic arrangements as well as the desire for a society that is more equal. On the other hand, it has also aroused great discussion and worry among many who believe that socialism, and Marxism in particular, is incompatible with American principles and as destructive to economic success and individual liberties.

In light of these factors, the investigation of the possible effects that socialism may have on the United States of America is not only an intellectual exercise; rather, it is an essential engagement with matters about the path that the nation will take in the future. It encourages a contemplative examination of the ways in which various ideologies may make policies, have an impact on cultural values, and have an impact on the lives of individuals in their day-to-day lives. In light of the fact that the United States of America is currently at a crossroads, it is essential to investigate the repercussions of adopting or rejecting socialist ideals in order to influence public discourse and policy decisions that will have an impact on the nation for many generations to come.

Theoretical Foundations

Marxism vs. Socialism vs. Capitalism

Marxism is an ideology based on Karl Marx and Friedrich Engels' works, particularly "The Communist Manifesto" (1848) and "Das Kapital" (1867). It argues for the historical inevitability of the proletariat's revolution against the bourgeoisie, leading to the abolition of class structures and the establishment of a communist society (Marx & Engels, 1848). In this society, the state's purpose is to wither away as class distinctions vanish, leaving a classless, stateless world where the community collectively owns production means (Engels, 1880).

Socialism encompasses a spectrum of ideologies advocating for the government or collective ownership of production means. Unlike Marxism's focus on class struggle and revolution, socialism includes both reformist and revolutionary perspectives, aiming to reduce economic inequalities through redistributive policies and social welfare (Bernstein, 1899). Socialists see the state as a central figure in redistributing resources to achieve social justice.

Capitalism is characterized by private property, market-based resource allocation, and the profit motive. Adam Smith's "The Wealth of Nations" (1776) provides the foundational framework for capitalism, emphasizing the benefits of a free market and competition for economic development and societal well-being. The state's role is primarily to protect property rights, enforce contracts, and maintain competition (Smith, 1776).

Historical Context

Soviet Union: The establishment of a Marxist-Leninist state following the 1917 Bolshevik Revolution marked a significant attempt to implement Marx's theories. The initial years saw rapid industrialization and improvements in literacy and healthcare, but eventually led to economic stagnation and the system's collapse in 1991 (Fitzpatrick, 1994).

China: Mao Zedong's China, from 1949 onwards, pursued a Marxist-Leninist path with significant achievements in social indicators. However, policies like the Great Leap Forward and the Cultural Revolution resulted in economic disaster and widespread human suffering. China's post-Mao economic reforms introduced elements of market capitalism, leading to unprecedented economic growth, though under strict political control (Meisner, 1999).

Scandinavian Countries: These nations exemplify a successful blend of market capitalism with extensive social welfare, often referred to as "social democracy." High standards of living, low income inequality, and robust social services characterize these countries, supported by comprehensive social welfare systems and high taxation (Esping-Andersen, 1990).

Cuba and Venezuela: Cuba, since the 1959 revolution, has achieved successes in healthcare and education but faces economic challenges exacerbated by U.S. sanctions. Venezuela under Chavez and Maduro saw initial improvements in social indicators, but recent years have been marked by economic crises and political instability, illustrating the pitfalls of resource-dependent socialism and autocratic governance (Corrales & Penfold, 2011).

The Divisive Strategies of Marxist Regimes

Marxist regimes have historically employed a variety of strategies to consolidate power and transform society according to their ideological objectives. Central to these strategies is the use of class struggle as a tool to create binary divisions within society, alongside the suppression of dissent through censorship, political persecution, and surveillance.

Class struggle as a tool

At the heart of Marxist theory is the concept of class struggle, which Karl Marx and Friedrich Engels identified as the driving force of historical development and social change. Marx posited that all human history is the history of class struggles, with society split into antagonistic classes: the bourgeoisie, who own the means of production, and the proletariat, the working class exploited under capitalism (Marx & Engels, 1848). Marxist regimes have used this dichotomy to foster a binary division within society, framing the political and social narrative as a battle between the oppressors (bourgeoisie) and the oppressed (proletariat).

This binary division serves several purposes:

Mobilization: It rallies the working class and other marginalized groups around the regime, using the promise of rectifying historical injustices and achieving social and economic equality.

Legitimization: By portraying themselves as champions of the proletariat, Marxist regimes seek to legitimize their rule and their radical policies as necessary for dismantling the capitalist system.

Delegitimization of Opponents: Anyone opposing the regime is labeled as a defender of the bourgeois class and, by extension, an enemy of the people.

The use of class struggle as a tool for societal division can be observed in the early Soviet Union, where the Bolsheviks implemented policies aimed at dismantling the bourgeoisie as a class, and in Mao Zedong's China, particularly during the Cultural Revolution, where class labels determined one's social status and level of persecution (Fitzpatrick, 1994; Meisner, 1999).

Suppression of Dissent

Marxist regimes have systematically suppressed dissent to maintain power and control over the societal transformation process. Methods of suppression include:

Censorship: Control over the media and the flow of information is a hallmark of Marxist regimes. The Soviet Union under Stalin and China under Mao exerted tight control over the press, literature, and the arts, ensuring that only state-approved messages were disseminated (Goldman, 2005). This control extended to education, where the curriculum was designed to indoctrinate citizens with Marxist-Leninist ideology.

Political Persecution: Individuals and groups perceived as threats to the regime's stability or ideological purity face arrest, imprisonment, or worse. The Gulag labor camps in the Soviet Union and the mass purges during the Cultural Revolution are stark examples of how political persecution was used to eliminate dissent (Applebaum, 2003; MacFarquhar & Schoenhals, 2006).

State Surveillance: Marxist regimes have employed extensive surveillance apparatuses to monitor citizens and identify potential dissent. The Stasi in East Germany is perhaps one of the most efficient examples of a surveillance state, with a vast network of informants and sophisticated spying techniques used to keep tabs on the populace (Gieseke, 2014).

These strategies of division and suppression have been critical in enabling Marxist regimes to attempt the radical restructuring of society. While they have arguably mobilized support and maintained control, they have also led to significant human rights abuses, economic dislocation, and the alienation of segments of the population. The legacy of these divisive strategies continues to inform contemporary debates about the viability and desirability of adopting Marxist principles in modern political contexts.

Identity Politics: A Tool for Further Division

Identity politics are used by Marxist governments and more generally by socialist movements. This is a strategic extension of the idea of a class struggle beyond just economic lines. This approach involves emphasizing and politicizing social identities based on race, ethnicity, gender, and sexuality, framing these identities within a narrative of oppression and resistance. While Marxism traditionally focuses on economic class struggle, the incorporation of identity politics has allowed contemporary Marxist and socialist movements to address a broader spectrum of inequalities and injustices in society.

Theoretical Basis

The theoretical basis for integrating identity politics into Marxist thought can be traced to the later developments in Marxist theory, particularly through the work of theorists like Antonio Gramsci and the Frankfurt School. Gramsci's concept of cultural hegemony suggested that the ruling class maintains control not just through economic means but also by dominating cultural and ideological institutions (Gramsci, 1971). This expanded our understanding of oppression and provided a framework for examining how various forms of identity-based inequalities are maintained through cultural and societal norms.

Utilization in Marxist Regimes and Movements

In practice, Marxist regimes and movements have utilized identity politics as a means to:

Broaden Appeal: By addressing a wide range of identity-based grievances, Marxist movements aim to build larger coalitions that transcend economic class divisions, appealing to individuals and groups that may feel marginalized or oppressed due to aspects of their identity beyond their class status.

Highlight Intersectionality: This approach acknowledges the interconnected nature of social categorizations and how overlapping systems of oppression affect those who are most marginalized in society. Many contemporary socialist movements have embraced it as a justification for a more nuanced approach to social justice that addresses sexism, racism, and other forms of discrimination (Crenshaw, 1989).

Divert Focus: Critics argue that the focus on identity politics can sometimes serve to divert attention from the core economic issues at the heart of Marxist critique, potentially fracturing solidarity among the working class by emphasizing differences over common economic interests.

Case Studies

While traditional Marxist regimes (e.g., the Soviet Union, Maoist China) primarily focused on class struggle, contemporary socialist movements and some socialist-leaning governments have increasingly adopted identity politics. For example:

Bolivarian Revolution in Venezuela: Hugo Chávez and Nicolás Maduro's governments have rhetorically embraced identity politics, highlighting indigenous rights and Afro-Venezuelan heritage as part of their socialist agenda, aiming to align their economic policies with broader social justice issues (Ellner, 2012).

Contemporary Socialist Movements: In Western democracies, socialist and progressive movements often incorporate identity politics into their platforms, advocating for policies that address systemic racism, gender inequality, and LGBTQ+ rights alongside economic reforms.

Critique and debate

The integration of identity politics into Marxist and socialist strategies has sparked significant debate.

Solidarity vs. Division: Proponents argue that addressing identity-based oppressions is essential for building a more just and equitable society, while critics within the left caution that it may dilute the focus on class struggle and economic inequality, hindering class solidarity.

Strategic Considerations: Some view the embrace of identity politics as a necessary evolution of Marxist theory to remain relevant in addressing contemporary social issues, while others see it as a departure from Marxist principles focused on class and economic structures.

The use of identity politics by Marxist regimes and movements reflects an attempt to engage with the complex realities of social injustice in the modern world. It represents both an expansion of Marxist critique to encompass a wider array of oppressions and a strategic choice that has generated considerable discussion and debate within and outside Marxist circles. The effectiveness and implications of this strategy continue to be a focal point of analysis for both supporters and critics of Marxism and socialism.

Economic Consequences

The adoption of Marxist and broader socialist policies, particularly wealth redistribution and central planning, poses significant economic consequences. While these policies aim to create a more equitable society by addressing income and wealth disparities, they can also lead to various economic inefficiencies, challenge the incentive structures that drive economic vitality, and distort market signals, resulting in shortages and surpluses.

Impact on Prosperity: Wealth Redistribution and Central Planning

Wealth Redistribution: Socialist policies often involve redistributing wealth from the more affluent sections of society to the less affluent through progressive taxation, social welfare programs, and other redistributive mechanisms. While these measures can reduce poverty and inequality in the short term, they can also dampen the incentives for wealth creation. High levels of taxation and redistribution can discourage entrepreneurship, investment, and risk-taking, which are critical drivers of economic growth and innovation (Okun, 1975).

Central Planning: Central planning, a hallmark of Marxist economic policy, entails government control over the allocation of resources, production, and distribution decisions. While intended to ensure a fair and equitable distribution of goods and services, central planning often leads to inefficiencies due to the impossibility of accurately determining consumer preferences, production costs, and other market dynamics from a centralized perspective. The Soviet Union's economic history illustrates how central planning can result in misallocations of resources, stifled innovation, and ultimately, economic stagnation (Kornai, 1992).

The Dilemma of Economic Equality

The pursuit of economic equality represents a fundamental goal of socialism, aiming to eliminate the class distinctions that Marxists view as inherently exploitative. However, this pursuit can conflict with the incentive structures that motivate individuals to work, innovate, and excel. In a system where wealth redistribution significantly reduces the financial benefits of higher productivity and innovation, there may be less motivation for individuals to invest in their education, work harder, or take entrepreneurial risks. This paradox highlights the delicate balance between achieving a more equitable distribution of wealth and maintaining the economic vitality necessary for a prosperous society (Hayek, 1944).

Market Distortion: The Effects of Socialist Policies

Socialist policies can also lead to significant market distortions as government interventions alter the natural mechanisms of supply and demand. Price controls, subsidies, and state monopolies, often implemented to make goods and services more accessible and to protect domestic industries, can create mismatches between supply and demand. For example, artificially low prices can lead to shortages, as seen with basic food items and housing in various socialist countries, while subsidies can lead to surpluses and inefficiencies, such as overproduction in certain sectors (Schumpeter, 1942).

These market distortions not only affect the availability of goods and services but also signal to producers and consumers in ways that do not reflect actual market conditions, leading to misallocations of resources and inefficiencies in the economy. Furthermore, the attempt to correct these distortions through further interventions often exacerbates the problems, leading to a cycle of increasing government control and decreasing market efficiency.

While socialist policies, including wealth redistribution and central planning, aim to create a more equitable society, they also present significant challenges to economic prosperity. The balancing act between fostering economic equality and maintaining incentive structures and market efficiency is a complex dilemma facing societies that pursue these policies. The historical and contemporary experiences of socialist and Marxist implementations provide valuable lessons on the potential economic consequences of such economic systems.

National Security Concerns

The adoption of socialist policies, especially those aligned with Marxist ideology, can have profound implications for a nation's national security posture, including the potential weakening of defense capabilities and shifts in foreign relations and international alliances.

Weakening of Defense

Reduced Defense Budgets: One of the key implications of socialist policies is the potential redirection of government spending from defense to social programs. Prioritizing welfare, healthcare, and education in the national budget can lead to reduced allocations for defense spending. While the aim of improving social welfare is commendable, excessively diminished defense budgets can undermine a country's military readiness and capabilities. This reduction can affect various aspects of national defense, from the maintenance of existing military hardware and the development of new technology to the training and preparedness of the armed forces (Perlo-Freeman & Sköns, 2008).

The weakening of defense capabilities is not merely a matter of reduced military strength but also affects a nation's strategic deterrence posture. Countries perceived as weakening militarily may become more vulnerable to external threats and less able to project power or fulfill their commitments to international security partnerships and alliances.

Strategic Implications: The strategic implications of reduced defense capabilities extend beyond the immediate risk of external aggression. They also include the potential loss of influence in international affairs. Military strength is a significant component of a nation's overall power projection, influencing its ability to negotiate, support allies, and participate in international peacekeeping efforts effectively (Brooks & Wohlforth, 2016).

Foreign Relations

Shift in Diplomatic Relations: Socialist policies, particularly those that emphasize anti-imperialism and solidarity with leftist movements worldwide, can lead to a reorientation of a nation's foreign policy. This shift may result in strained relations with traditionally allied countries, especially those with capitalist economies. For instance, the alignment of a socialist government with other socialist or authoritarian regimes, in opposition to neoliberal economic policies, can create diplomatic tensions and lead to a realignment of international alliances (Waltz, 1979).

Impact on International Alliances: The ideological underpinnings of socialist policies may also impact a country's participation in international alliances, particularly those with a strong emphasis on collective defense and economic cooperation among capitalist countries. For example, a socialist government may be less inclined to contribute to collective defense initiatives that are perceived as serving the interests of capitalist hegemony, leading to frictions within alliances like NATO or economic cooperatives like the European Union (EU) (Keohane, 1984).

Moreover, the promotion of socialist policies and rhetoric critical of neoliberalism and imperialism can resonate with other nations and movements, fostering solidarity among countries and groups with similar ideological leanings. While this can lead to new alliances, it also risks isolating the country from the global economic system and international community, potentially leading to economic sanctions, trade embargoes, and diplomatic isolation.

The interplay between socialist policies and national security concerns highlights the complex trade-offs that governments face in balancing domestic priorities with international obligations and strategic interests. The implications for defense capabilities and foreign relations underscore the need for careful consideration of the broader consequences of significant shifts in policy orientation.

Cultural Transformation

The implementation of socialist policies, particularly under Marxist regimes, has profound implications for cultural transformation, affecting national identity, cultural values, and the expression of arts and religion. These policies often aim to reshape society's cultural landscape to align with socialist ideals, leading to significant changes in how cultural identity is constructed and expressed.

Impact on Cultural Identity

Reshaping National Identity: Socialist policies frequently emphasize collective identity over individualism, seeking to create a sense of unity and solidarity among the populace. This collective identity is often constructed around the values of equality, social justice, and the rejection of capitalist exploitation. In Marxist contexts, the promotion of proletarian culture and values is intended to supplant bourgeois culture, which is seen as perpetuating class divisions and capitalist exploitation (Eagleton, 2006).

The transformation of national identity under socialism can involve the redefinition of historical narratives, where the history of class struggle and the contributions of socialist movements to national liberation or economic development are emphasized. This reimagining of national history serves not only to legitimize the current regime but also to foster a shared sense of purpose and direction among the citizenry.

Cultural Values: The promotion of socialist cultural values can lead to a shift in societal priorities and norms. Values such as cooperation, solidarity, and community welfare may take precedence over individual achievement, competition, and material success. While these changes can promote social cohesion and a focus on collective well-being, they may also suppress diversity of thought and the valorization of individual contributions to society and culture.

Censorship of the Arts and Suppression of Religion

Censorship of the Arts: Marxist regimes have often viewed the arts as a powerful medium for ideological expression and social commentary. As such, the arts under socialism are frequently subject to state control and censorship, with the aim of ensuring that they promote socialist values and contribute to the ideological education of the populace. This control can stifle artistic creativity and limit the diversity of artistic expression, as works that critique the regime or deviate from socialist realism—the official artistic style of the Soviet Union—are censored or suppressed (Golomstock, 1990).

The suppression of artistic freedom under the guise of promoting socially beneficial content reflects a broader tension within socialism between the desire for cultural flourishing and the perceived need to guard against bourgeois and counter-revolutionary influences.

Suppression of Religion: Many Marxist regimes have adopted an atheistic stance, viewing religion as an opiate of the masses that perpetuates illusion and impedes the realization of a truly socialist society (Marx, 1843). Consequently, socialist policies often involve the suppression of religious practices, the closure or repurposing of religious institutions, and the promotion of secularism as a core component of socialist identity.

The suppression of religion under Marxist regimes not only seeks to eliminate a potential source of opposition but also aims to reshape cultural identity around secular, socialist principles. However, such policies can alienate religious communities, lead to cultural and spiritual impoverishment, and ignite resistance among those for whom religious belief and practice are central to their identity and way of life.

The cultural transformation under socialist policies, particularly within Marxist regimes, reveals the complex interplay between ideology, cultural identity, and the arts. While aiming to create a cohesive national identity rooted in socialist values, such policies can also lead to the suppression of diversity, creativity, and religious freedom, illustrating the challenges of balancing ideological goals with cultural and spiritual richness.

Safeguarding Heritage

In the discourse surrounding the implementation of socialist policies, particularly those inspired by Marxist ideology, a crucial consideration is the safeguarding of a nation's heritage. This encompasses the preservation of cultural traditions, economic freedoms, and political liberties. The challenge lies in balancing the pursuit of social justice with the protection of individual rights and liberties, ensuring that efforts to address inequality do not erode the foundational values that underpin a vibrant, democratic society.

The importance of preserving traditions

Cultural Traditions: Cultural heritage and traditions are the lifeblood of a nation, providing a sense of identity, continuity, and belonging for its people. The preservation of cultural traditions is essential not only for maintaining the diversity of human expression but also for fostering social cohesion and intergenerational solidarity. Socialist policies must, therefore, be mindful of the ways in which they seek to transform society, ensuring that the valorization of collective identity does not come at the expense of cultural diversity and the rich tapestry of individual expression that characterizes a nation's heritage (Hobsbawm & Ranger, 1983).

Economic Freedoms: Economic freedom, including the rights to property, free enterprise, and innovation, is a cornerstone of dynamic and prosperous societies. While socialist policies aim to rectify economic inequalities, it is vital to ensure that such interventions do not stifle entrepreneurship, innovation, and the individual initiative that drive economic progress and improvement in living standards. Preserving economic freedoms requires a regulatory and policy framework that balances wealth redistribution with incentives for economic contribution and innovation (Friedman, 1962).

Political Liberties: Political freedoms, such as freedom of speech, assembly, and participation in the democratic process, are fundamental to the functioning of a democratic society. These liberties allow for the expression of diverse viewpoints, the peaceful resolution of societal conflicts, and the accountability of government actions to the populace. Socialist policies should strengthen rather than diminish these political liberties, ensuring that efforts to achieve social justice are conducted within a framework that respects and promotes political pluralism and the rule of law (Dahl, 1989).

Balancing social justice with individual liberties

The pursuit of social justice is a noble and essential endeavor aimed at creating a more equitable and fair society. However, achieving this goal without undermining individual liberties presents a complex challenge. The key lies in recognizing that social justice and individual freedoms are not mutually exclusive but are, in fact, complementary.

Policy Considerations: Effective social policies should aim to lift the most vulnerable members of society, providing them with the opportunities and resources needed to achieve their potential without imposing undue restrictions on individual freedoms. This involves crafting policies that address the root causes of inequality and exclusion, such as access to education, healthcare, and economic opportunities, while respecting individual rights and freedoms (Sen, 1999).

Civic Engagement: Encouraging civic engagement and participation in policy-making processes ensures that diverse perspectives are considered and that policies reflect the needs and aspirations of a broader society. This participatory approach strengthens democracy, fosters a sense of collective responsibility, and ensures that the pursuit of social justice is aligned with the preservation of individual liberties (Putnam, 2000).

Safeguarding heritage while pursuing social justice requires a delicate balance between collective goals and individual rights. It necessitates a nuanced understanding of the complex interplay between social policies, cultural identity, economic freedom, and political liberties. By prioritizing policies that are inclusive, participatory, and respectful of diversity and individual rights, societies can move towards a more equitable and just future without compromising the rich heritage and foundational values that define them.

Conclusion: A Critical Crossroads

As the United States stands at a pivotal juncture in its political and economic discourse, the consideration of adopting socialist policies presents both significant opportunities and profound challenges. This exploration has delved into the complexities of socialist and Marxist ideologies, their impact on society's economic, political, and cultural landscapes, and the delicate balance between promoting social justice and preserving foundational freedoms. The potential risks and challenges of embracing such policies necessitate a nuanced and informed debate about the nation's future direction.

Summarizing the risks and challenges

Economic Implications: The adoption of socialist policies could lead to economic inefficiencies, including diminished incentives for innovation and entrepreneurship, potential misallocation of resources through central planning, and market distortions leading to shortages and surpluses. While aiming to address income inequality and provide universal access to essential services, these policies might also challenge the dynamism that characterizes the U.S. economy (Friedman, 1962; Hayek, 1944).

Political and Cultural Considerations: The implementation of socialist principles could also impact the political and cultural fabric of the United States. The emphasis on collective identity and social justice might challenge the deeply ingrained values of individualism and personal freedom. Moreover, the suppression of dissent, censorship of the arts, and potential curtailment of religious freedoms under more authoritarian socialist regimes provide cautionary tales for the preservation of democratic principles and cultural diversity (Dahl, 1989; Hobsbawm & Ranger, 1983).

National Security and International Relations: On the global stage, a shift towards socialism could alter the United States' foreign policy, defense spending priorities, and its role in international alliances. These changes could have ramifications for national security, geopolitical stability, and the country's ability to project power and influence internationally (Waltz, 1979; Brooks & Wohlforth, 2016).

The Importance of Informed Debate and Careful Consideration

The consideration of socialist policies in the United States underscores the importance of informed debate and careful deliberation. As the nation contemplates its future path, it is imperative to engage in a robust and nuanced discussion that encompasses a wide range of perspectives and disciplines. Policymakers, scholars, and the public must critically assess the potential benefits and drawbacks of socialist policies, drawing on historical experiences and contemporary analyses to inform their viewpoints.

Balancing Act: Achieving a balance between addressing the legitimate concerns of inequality, access to healthcare, education, and social welfare while preserving economic competitiveness, individual freedoms, and democratic governance is paramount. This balance requires a thoughtful approach to policy-making that considers the long-term implications of significant ideological shifts.

Future Path: As the United States stands at this critical crossroads, the decisions made today will shape the legacy left for future generations. It is through informed debate, democratic engagement, and a commitment to the principles of liberty, equality, and justice that the nation can navigate the complexities of the 21st century, ensuring a prosperous, inclusive, and vibrant future for all its citizens.

In conclusion, the exploration of socialism's potential impact on America highlights the need for a comprehensive understanding of the trade-offs involved. By fostering an inclusive and informed public discourse, the United States can chart a course that reflects its values, addresses its challenges, and secures a prosperous future for generations to come.

References

Applebaum, A. (2003). Gulag: A History. Doubleday.

Bernstein, E. (1899). The Preconditions of Socialism. Cambridge University Press.

Brooks, S. G., & Wohlforth, W. C. (2016). America Abroad: The United States' Global Role in the 21st Century. Oxford University Press.

Corrales, J., & Penfold, M. (2011). Dragon in the Tropics: Hugo Chavez and the Political Economy of Revolution in Venezuela. Brookings Institution Press.

Crenshaw, K. (1989). "Demarginalizing the Intersection of Race and Sex: A Black Feminist Critique of Antidiscrimination Doctrine, Feminist Theory and Antiracist Politics." University of Chicago Legal Forum, Vol. 1989, Issue 1, Article 8.

Dahl, R. A. (1989). Democracy and Its Critics. Yale University Press.

Ellner, S. (2012). "The Distinguishing Features of Latin America's New Left in Power: The Chávez, Morales, and Correa Governments." Latin American Perspectives, Vol. 39, No. 1, pp. 96-114.

Eagleton, T. (2006). Ideology: An Introduction. Verso Books.

Engels, F. (1880). Socialism: Utopian and Scientific. Progress Publishers.

Esping-Andersen, G. (1990). The Three Worlds of Welfare Capitalism. Princeton University Press.

Fitzpatrick, S. (1994). The Russian Revolution. Oxford University Press.

Friedman, M. (1962). Capitalism and Freedom. University of Chicago Press.

Gieseke, J. (2014). The History of the Stasi: East Germany's Secret Police, 1945-1990. Berghahn Books.

Goldman, M. (2005). Karl Marx, His Life and Environment. Oxford University Press.

Golomstock, I. (1990). Totalitarian Art in the Soviet Union, the Third Reich, Fascist Italy and the People's Republic of China. HarperCollins.

Gramsci, A. (1971). "Selections from the Prison Notebooks." International Publishers.

Hayek, F. A. (1944). The Road to Serfdom. University of Chicago Press.

Hobsbawm, E., & Ranger, T. (Eds.). (1983). The Invention of Tradition. Cambridge University Press.

Keohane, R. O. (1984). After Hegemony: Cooperation and Discord in the World Political Economy. Princeton University Press.

Kornai, J. (1992). The Socialist System: The Political Economy of Communism. Princeton University Press.

MacFarquhar, R., & Schoenhals, M. (2006). Mao's Last Revolution. Harvard University Press.

Marx, K., & Engels, F. (1848). The Communist Manifesto. Penguin Books.

Meisner, M. (1999). Mao's China and After: A History of the People's Republic. Free Press.

Okun, A. M. (1975). Equality and Efficiency: The Big Tradeoff. Brookings Institution Press.

Perlo-Freeman, S., & Sköns, E. (2008). "The Impact of Economic Crises on Global Military Expenditure." SIPRI Yearbook. Stockholm International Peace Research Institute.

Putnam, R. D. (2000). Bowling Alone: The Collapse and Revival of American Community. Simon & Schuster.

Schumpeter, J. A. (1942). Capitalism, Socialism and Democracy. Harper & Brothers.

Sen, A. (1999). Development as Freedom. Oxford University Press.

Smith, A. (1776). The Wealth of Nations. W. Strahan and T. Cadell, London.

Waltz, K. N. (1979). Theory of International Politics. Addison-Wesley.

Chapter 1: The Rise of Radical Leftist Elitist Groups

THE SILENT SUBVERSION

Chapter 1 delves into the emergence of radical leftist elitist groups in the United States. As we delve into the underbelly of society, we discover how these groups are gaining traction and advocating for the establishment of a Socialist-State. Through their clandestine plans and plots, they aim to tear the fabric of American democracy and undermine the very foundation of the nation.

Chapter Outline:

1. Introduction

2. The Rise of Leftist Elites

3. The Socialist- State Agenda

4. The Marxist Mindset

5. The Subversion Conspiracy

6. The Liberal Agenda

7. The Liberal Love-Hate Relationship with America

8. The Impact on Society

9. Conclusion

Introduction: The Silent Subversion

The annals of United States history are replete with periods of triumph and adversity, reflecting the enduring spirit of freedom, liberty, and the pursuit of opportunity that has defined the nation since its inception. Celebrated as a land of dreams, the U.S. has historically been a beacon for those seeking to achieve greatness through diligence, innovation, and personal freedom. From the founding fathers' Declaration of Independence to significant events like the fight for women's suffrage, the abolition of slavery, and the defense of democracy during the Cold War, its legacy is filled with outstanding accomplishments. Yet, amidst these landmarks of progress, the nation has navigated the turbulent waters of ideological shifts, political dissent, and internal strife.

Within the tapestry of these internal conflicts lies the thread of a more insidious challenge: the silent subversion by extreme leftist elitist groups. Operating beneath the veneer of everyday life, these groups have gradually woven a narrative that threatens the very bedrock of American democratic principles. This subversion is not a frontal assault but a creeping infiltration, aiming to dismantle the foundational structures of society from within.

The United States, hailed as a crucible of opportunity and innovation, now faces a critical examination of its internal dynamics. Questions arise about the forces undermining democratic governance, the genesis and proliferation of extreme leftist ideologies, and their covert agenda to establish a socialist state. This chapter embarks on a journey to unravel the growth of these movements, shedding light on their philosophies and strategies and the existential threat they pose to the American democratic fabric.

Our exploration delves into the intellectual origins and ambitions of these leftist groups, dissecting their socialist-state agenda and the Marxist ethos that fuels their vision. We will navigate the complex networks of subversive activities that enable their surreptitious influence on American culture and politics, examining their intricate ties to the broader liberal agenda and the paradoxical relationship they maintain with the nation they seek to transform.

Furthermore, we will assess the impact of these extreme leftist factions on American society, understanding how their doctrines, rhetoric, and actions have eroded traditional values, undermined individual liberties, and weakened the free-market system. However, this narrative is not solely one of dissent and subversion but also of resistance and resilience. We will witness the awakening of a silent majority, a diverse coalition united against the threat these groups pose, and their concerted effort to safeguard the nation's future.

The ensuing chapters will not only chronicle the ideological battlefields but also project the potential outcomes of this conflict. We will explore the ramifications of a successful socialist agenda on the economy, national security, and the cherished freedoms and values that have defined the American way of life. It is a call to action for every American to reclaim their destiny and ensure the preservation of the nation's legacy for future generations.

As we navigate "The Silent Subversion," we will traverse the intricate web of ideology, politics, and dissent, exploring the experiences of supporters and critics alike. This journey is an invitation to challenge assumptions, illuminate the complexities of contemporary American society, and empower citizens to make informed decisions about their nation's future. Through rigorous research, compelling narratives, and expert insights, "The Silent Subversion" seeks to unearth the roots of this covert movement and its profound implications for the United States.

References

Tocqueville, A. de. (1835). Democracy in America. Harper Perennial Modern Classics.

Friedman, M. (1962). Capitalism and freedom University of Chicago Press.

Hobsbawm, E. (1994). The Age of Extremes: The Short Twentieth Century, 1914–1991 Pantheon Books.

Huntington, S. P. (1996). The Clash of Civilizations and the Remaking of World Order. Simon & Schuster.

Kendi, I. X. (2016). Stamped from the Beginning: The Definitive History of Racist Ideas in America. Nation Books.Part 2: The Rise of Leftist Elites

The Rise of Leftist Elites

A Changing Political Landscape

The emergence and consolidation of leftist elites within the broader context of shifting ideologies has marked the transformation of the American political landscape. This change reflects a departure from traditional political discourse, incorporating more progressive and leftist viewpoints into mainstream political debate.

The Democratic Party, historically a tapestry of various ideological strands, has witnessed a notable shift towards progressive ideals, influenced significantly by leftist elites. This evolution is evident in the rise of figures like Senator Bernie Sanders and Representative Alexandria Ocasio-Cortez, who have championed progressive agendas such as the Green New Deal, universal healthcare, and income inequality reduction (Issenberg, 2020; Klein, 2020).

The Intersection of Ideology and Elitism

Leftist elites, characterized by their amalgamation of progressive values and significant societal influence, have utilized their resources to amplify their ideological stances. Individuals like George Soros have been pivotal, using their wealth to support progressive causes and candidates, thereby shaping the political and social discourse (Soros, 2019).

The influence of these elites extends beyond financial contributions, permeating academia, the media, and cultural spheres. They leverage their positions to influence public opinion, advocating for progressive policies and ideas. The digital era has further empowered these elites, enabling direct engagement with the public and bypassing traditional media gatekeepers (Tufecki, 2017).

The Influence of Academia

Academic institutions have become arenas where leftist ideologies have flourished, particularly within the humanities and social sciences. Critical theories, including critical race theory and feminist theory, have gained prominence, shaping scholarly and student discourse on power dynamics and social hierarchies (Delgado & Stefancic, 2017).

The Role of Media

Leftist elites have had a significant impact on the media landscape because they are journalists, commentators, and influencers who help to shape national discussions of important issues. The rise of digital platforms has democratized information dissemination, allowing progressive voices to reach wider audiences directly (Couldry & Mejias, 2019).

Elitism and Cultural Influence

Cultural sectors, including Hollywood and the arts, have seen an increased presence of leftist ideologies. Artists and celebrities use their platforms to advocate for social and political change, influencing public perceptions and discussions on societal issues (Dyer, 2019).

Conclusion

The ascent of leftist elites in the U.S. reflects a complex interplay of ideological commitment and societal influence. Their impact on the political, academic, media, and cultural spheres has significantly shaped public discourse, contributing to a more progressive national conversation. However, this rise has also sparked debates about the role of elitism in politics and the balance between progressive ideals and broader societal acceptance.

References

Couldry, N., & Mejias, U. A. (2019). The Costs of Connection: How Data Is Colonizing Human Life and Appropriating It for Capitalism. Stanford University Press.

Delgado, R., & Stefancic, J. (2017). Critical Race Theory: An Introduction. New York University Press.

Dyer, R. (2019). Stars. British Film Institute.
Issenberg, S. (2020). The Victory Lab: The Secret Science of Winning Campaigns. Crown Publishing Group.

Klein, E. (2020). Why We're Polarized. Simon & Schuster.
Soros, G. (2019). In Defense of Open Society: Public Affairs

Tufecki, Z. (2017). Twitter and Tear Gas: The Power and Fragility of Networked Protests Yale University Press.

Part 3: The Socialist-State Agenda

Throughout the course of our investigation into the growth of extreme leftist elitist groups in the United States, we have dissected the various levels of their ideology and the rise to prominence that they have experienced. As we move forward, we will delve even more into their ultimate goal, which is the formation of a socialist state. This lofty and disputed objective serves as the driving force behind their covert plans and activities, and it is at the heart of their organizational movement. To comprehend the repercussions of this agenda, it is necessary to first investigate the fundamental principles of socialism and how these principles are expressed within the setting of the United States.

The Socialist Ideology

Socialism, as an ideology, advocates for collective ownership and control of the means of production and distribution. The concept that money and resources ought to be divided more equally throughout the population, to decrease or eliminate socio-economic differences, is the foundation by which it is understood. The pursuit of a society in which the state plays a key role in organizing and regulating economic activity is the common thread that runs through all instances of socialism, although socialism can take many different shapes and mean different things.

A Historical Perspective

It is possible to trace the origins of socialist ideology back to the 19th century when significant authors like as Karl Marx and Friedrich

Engels laid the intellectual groundwork for the ideological framework. In their fundamental book, "The Communist Manifesto" (1848), they advocated for the downfall of capitalist institutions and the construction of a society without classes in which the state would gradually disappear. This vision, albeit utopian, sparked the imaginations of a great number of people and resulted in the formation of socialist groups all over the world.

Varieties of Socialism

It is essential to bring to your attention the fact that socialism is not a singular philosophy. It has, with time, fragmented into some different schools of thought, each of which has its own vision of how a socialist society needs to operate differently. Many want a gradual change by democratic means, while others argue for more revolutionary approaches. Different forms of socialism have emerged as a result of the diversity that exists within the socialist ideology. These models include democratic socialism, social democracy, and communism, each of which has distinct characteristics and goals.

The Socialist-State Agenda in the United States, Historical Context

There is a long and complicated history of socialist beliefs and activities in the United States of America. Although the United States has, for the most part, adhered to a capitalist economic structure, there have been specific eras in American history in which socialist ideals have found a healthy home. The beginning of the 20th century was marked by the establishment of socialist parties and labor organizations, which were influenced by socialist beliefs that were prevalent across the world. Aiming to solve concerns of social justice, workers' rights, and economic inequality, these movements sought to address these issues.

Contemporary Resurgence

Over the past several years, there has been a revival of socialist rhetoric inside the political discourse of the United States. Individuals of significant influence, such as Bernie Sanders and Alexandria Ocasio-Cortez, have publicly acknowledged their affiliation with democratic socialists and have earned a significant amount of support, particularly among younger generations. There is a drive toward more broad government interference in the economy, which is reflected in their policy ideas, which include universal healthcare, free higher education, and taxation of wealth.

The Goals of the Socialist-State Agenda

Economic Redistribution: At the heart of the socialist-state agenda is the idea of redistributing wealth and resources to reduce socio-economic disparities. Advocates contend that the existing capitalist system is responsible for the perpetuation of economic inequality, and they attempt to bring about a solution to this problem by implementing policies such as progressive taxation, universal basic income, and social safety nets (Piketty, 2014).

Expanding Government Control: Socialism entails a more significant role for the state in economic planning and regulation. This involves the nationalization of important sectors, the expansion of labor rights, and the establishment of healthcare and educational systems that are funded by the government. The goal is to ensure that all people have equal access to vital services and to offer such services to all residents.

Addressing Climate Change: Many proponents of the socialist-state agenda prioritize environmental concerns. To tackle climate change, they argue for forceful government engagement, with a particular focus on the transition to renewable energy sources, tougher environmental legislation, and sustainable development practices.

Worker Empowerment: Socialism places a strong emphasis on workers' rights and collective bargaining. Increasing the minimum wage, strengthening labor unions, and ensuring that working conditions are fair are all goals of the agenda document. With this, we want to achieve a more equitable distribution of power between employers and employees.

Universal Healthcare: Access to healthcare is a central theme in the socialist-state agenda. The provision of medical care ought to be a basic right, rather than a privilege, according to proponents. They advocate for the establishment of a healthcare system that is solely funded by a single-payer, which is often known as "Medicare for All."

The Controversy Surrounding the Agenda

Within American culture, the socialist state program has provoked a very heated discussion. On the other hand, proponents believe that it solves urgent problems such as the unequal distribution of money, the lack of access to healthcare, and the impending climate disaster. The argument that they are making is that it is consistent with the concepts of social justice and economic justness.

Critics, on the other hand, raise several concerns:

Economic Viability: Skeptics question the economic feasibility of extensive government intervention and redistribution. According to their argument, it has the potential to hinder innovation, inhibit entrepreneurial endeavors, and lead to inefficiencies in the allocation of resources.

Individual Freedom: Critics express concerns about the potential erosion of individual freedoms in a more centrally planned economy. Some people believe that substantial government control may restrict individual options and make it more difficult for individuals to take initiative.

Market Impact: The socialist-state agenda could have significant ramifications for markets and businesses. There is a concern among critics that additional regulation and taxation might discourage investment and the development of new jobs.

Budgetary Challenges: Implementing policies like universal healthcare and free education would require substantial government expenditure. Some individuals express their worries about the long-term viability of such projects and the potential burden they may impose on subsequent generations.

Political Polarization: The debate over socialism has contributed to political polarization in the United States. Over time, it has evolved into a contentious matter, with individuals on both extremes of the spectrum frequently remaining steadfast in their stances.

The Path Forward

As the United States grapples with the implications of the socialist-state agenda, it finds itself at a crossroads. The decisions that are taken in the years to come will have a significant impact on the socio-economic environment and political discourse of the nation.

It is of the utmost importance for the people of the United States to engage in a conversation that is both well-informed and constructive on the role of the government, the equilibrium between individual liberty and communal responsibility, and the most effective future course of action for the nation. The road ahead is marked by challenges, uncertainties, and differing visions for America's future, but it is also an opportunity for democracy to flourish and adapt to the evolving needs of society.

In subsequent chapters, we will explore the impact of this agenda on various aspects of American life, including national security, individual freedoms, and cultural values. We will be able to traverse the complicated landscape of the 21st century in the United States of America with clarity and purpose if we have a full awareness of the socialist-state agenda and the probable implications of its implementation.

References:

Piketty, T. (2014). Capital in the Twenty-First Century. Harvard University Press.

13

Part 4: The Marxist Mindset

In our journey through the underbelly of radical leftist elitist groups and their quest to establish a socialist state, we now arrive at the intellectual cornerstone of their ideology—the Marxist mindset. To comprehend the allure and implications of this mindset, we must delve into the origins, principles, and historical context of Marxism.

The Genesis of Marxism

A sociopolitical and economic theory that serves as the foundation for a wide variety of leftist groups all over the world is known as Marxism. This theory was named after its inventor, Karl Marx (1818-1883). Marx, in collaboration with Friedrich Engels, principally developed his views in two seminal writings: "The Communist Manifesto" (1848) and "Das Kapital" (Capital, 1867). Both of these publications were considered to be groundbreaking.

The Historical Context

It is vital to have a solid understanding of the historical context of the 19th century to comprehend Marxism. European society was undergoing profound changes as a result of the Industrial Revolution, which was in full swing. The tremendous industrialization and urbanization that occurred during this time and the establishment of a clear class division between the bourgeoisie (the capitalist class) and the proletariat (the working class) were the defining characteristics of this period.

The Class Struggle

Marxism is based on the idea that there is a conflict between different classes. Marx thought that history might be seen as a series of class battles, with each stage being characterized by the predominance of one class over another. He anticipated that the last step of this historical evolution would end in the triumph of the proletariat over the bourgeoisie, which would lead to the foundation of a society without classes, which would be a communist paradise.

Economic Determinism

Marxism is often described as dialectical materialism—a philosophy that interprets history through the lens of economic forces. Marx proposed that the social and political structures of a society were defined by economic ties, and more specifically by the ownership of the means of production. He contended that capitalism necessarily resulted in working conditions that were characterized by inequality, exploitation, and alienation.

Key Tenets of Marxism

To comprehend the Marxist mindset, it is vital to examine its key tenets:

1. Historical Materialism: Marxism posits that historical development is driven by changes in the mode of production. Capitalism succeeded feudalism, and Marx believed that capitalism would eventually lead to communism. Feudalism was replaced by capitalism. From the

perspective of historical materialism, the progression of society is inextricably tied to the many economic changes that occur.

2. Class Struggle: Central to Marxism is the belief that society is divided into two primary classes: the bourgeoisie (owners of the means of production) and the proletariat (working class). The struggle between these classes, which is fueled by the capitalist exploitation of labor, is considered to be the driving force behind the transformation of historical events.

3. Means of Production: Marxism places significant emphasis on the means of production, which includes land, factories, and tools. Both the power dynamics and the economic ties within a society are shaped by the control and ownership of these particular tools.

4. Alienation: Marx argued that capitalism alienates workers from the products of their labor, from the production process itself, from their fellow workers, and their true human nature. He thought that this estrangement was a factor that led to the dehumanization of the working class.

5. Revolution: Marxist theory anticipates a proletarian revolution. Marxism is a political ideology that advocates for the working class to rise against the capitalists, abolish the capitalist system, and seize control of the means of production. This would lay the groundwork for the transition to socialism, which would eventually ultimately lead to communism.

Contemporary Relevance

The fundamental principles of Marxism continue to have an impact on leftist groups and political ideologies all over the world, although Marxism has developed and fragmented into many other schools of thought. In the context of the United States, the rebirth of Marxism may be seen in the language and policies that are espoused by certain parts of the left.

Critiques and Controversies

The Marxist way of thinking has been subjected to a large amount of criticism and debate, even though it continues to be appealing to certain individuals. According to critics, there are various concerns:

Economic Feasibility

The Marxist economic theories, according to skeptics, are intrinsically faulty and cannot be implemented in practice. Collective ownership of the means of production, according to their argument, might result in inefficiency, a reduction in creativity, and a lack of incentives for hard effort.

Individual Freedom

Concerns have been raised by critics over the possibility that a Marxist society might restrict the freedoms of specific individuals. According to their argument, a significant amount of governmental control has the potential to inhibit personal initiative and freedom of choice.

Historical Failures

The historical record includes instances where attempts to implement Marxist principles led to authoritarian regimes and economic hardships. Those who are opposed to Marxism believe that these failures demonstrate how Marxism cannot be implemented in real life.

Ideological Polarization

The resurgence of Marxist ideas has contributed to ideological polarization in American society. Several contentious problems have emerged, including debates over the role of the government, the appropriate balance between private and community interests, and the practicability of socialist programs.

Conclusion

The Marxist mindset represents a foundational element of many leftist movements and ideologies. The historical backdrop, core beliefs, and present relevance of this work shed light on the intellectual foundations upon which extreme leftist elitist groups in the United States are currently operating. We must acknowledge the ongoing legacy of Marxist thinking and the role it has played in molding the political landscape as we continue to unravel its agenda and the consequences it has for American society.

In the subsequent parts of this chapter, we will delve deeper into the subversion conspiracy, the liberal agenda, and the complex relationship between left-leaning ideologies and the United States.

References:

Marx, K., & Engels, F. (1848). The Communist Manifesto. London: League of the Just.

Part 5: The Subversion Conspiracy

In our journey through the clandestine world of radical leftist elitist groups, we encounter a web of covert machinations and hidden intentions—an aspect we aptly refer to as the subversion conspiracy. The purpose of this aspect of our inquiry is to shed light on the clandestine techniques that these groups use to achieve their cause of creating a socialist state in the United States of America.

The Veiled Agenda

At the heart of the subversion conspiracy lies a meticulously concealed agenda. Because these extreme leftist elite groups are aware that their goals might not connect with the general American population, they choose to operate in the shadows, away from the scrutiny of mainstream debate.

Their subversive tactics involve:

1. Infiltration of Key Institutions: One of the primary strategies employed by these groups is the infiltration of key institutions within American society (Knight, 2015). Academic institutions, the media, political groups, and even certain business enterprises are included in this category. By putting their supporters and agents in positions of power, they can gradually but successfully shift these institutions in the direction of their socialist objective.

2. Covert Funding: Financial resources play a crucial role in advancing any agenda (Gentry & Sjoberg, 2013). There is a widespread belief that

radical leftist elitist groups are known to channel money via a convoluted network of organizations, which makes it difficult to identify the origins of their financial support. Because of this, they can carry out their operations in a covert manner, avoiding the limelight that may disclose their genuine aims.

3. Manipulation of Public Opinion: To achieve their goals, these groups employ sophisticated propaganda and information warfare tactics. To influence public opinion and the dissemination of their narratives, they make use of media venues that are favorable to their cause. Among them include the propagation of false information and the vilification of perspectives that are in opposition to mainstream beliefs.

4. Subtle Policy Advocacy: Rather than openly championing their socialist agenda, these groups often advocate for policies that, on the surface, appear benign but serve to advance their objectives incrementally. By adopting this method of gradual implementation, they can avoid setting off alarm bells among the general population.

The Role of Ideological Indoctrination

Central to the subversion conspiracy is the indoctrination of individuals sympathetic to their cause. According to Knight (2015), this entails the dissemination of communist beliefs within educational institutions as well as other areas of influence. To achieve the desired change of society, the objective is to assemble a group of people who will advocate for the socialist cause from the inside and are committed to working toward its realization.

Historical Parallels

The subversion conspiracy is not a novel concept in history. Several other ideological forces, notably communism, utilized comparable strategies throughout the entirety of the 20th century to infiltrate and undermine democratic democracies. During the time of the Cold War, for example, communist regimes made significant efforts to exert influence and control Western institutions (Gentry & Sjoberg, 2013).

Countering the Subversion Conspiracy

Detecting and countering the subversion conspiracy pose significant challenges. It is necessary for there to be a society that is watchful and aware of the hidden strategies that are utilized by extreme leftist elitist individuals. A few examples of countermeasures against such subversion are as follows:

1. Transparency: Promoting transparency in political and institutional processes can help expose covert activities. Openness and accountability are two qualities that must be maintained by institutions at all times.

2. Media Literacy: Educating the public on media literacy is crucial to discerning accurate information from propaganda. Fact-checking and critical thinking are two examples of talents that fall under this category.

3. Protecting Democratic Values: Upholding democratic values, including freedom of speech and expression, is vital in safeguarding against subversion. When a society places a high emphasis on open debate and a variety of ideas, it is less likely to be susceptible to ideological manipulation.

Conclusion

The subversion conspiracy within radical leftist elitist groups represents a covert underbelly of activities aimed at fundamentally transforming the United States into a socialist state. These groups operate in secrecy, employing infiltration, covert funding, manipulation of public opinion, and ideological indoctrination to advance their agenda. It is becoming increasingly clear that the fight for the future of the United States of America is not at all transparent as we continue to dive further into the complicated web of their strategies and investigate the liberal agenda in the upcoming section of this chapter.

References:

Gentry, J. S., & Sjoberg, L. (2013). The Soviet Estimate: U.S. Intelligence Analysis & Russian Military Strength. Routledge.

Knight, A. (2015). The Making of the Cold War Enemy: Culture and Politics in the Military-Intellectual Complex. Princeton University Press.

Part 6: The Liberal Agenda

As our investigation into the emergence of extreme leftist elitist groups and their pursuit of a socialist-state agenda continues, we now turn our attention to a significant facet of their philosophy and impact—the liberal agenda. Although it is standard practice to use the terms "liberal" and "leftist" interchangeably, these terms refer to two separate political stances that frequently interact with one another. To get a thorough grasp of the liberal agenda within the larger framework of radical leftist elitism, it is vital to dive into this element, which will throw light on the complex forces that are molding American culture and politics.

Defining the Liberal Agenda

To have a complete understanding of the liberal agenda and the part it played in the development of radical leftist elitist groups, it is essential to have a clear definition of liberalism within the context of the political landscape in the United States.

Liberalism as a Political Philosophy

According to Locke (1689), liberalism is a political theory that emphasizes individual rights, liberty, and equality before the law. It is founded on the principle that governments need to safeguard and maintain the rights and liberties of the people who live under their jurisdiction. Throughout human history, liberalism has been an important factor in the formation of democratic societies. It has been a strong advocate for principles such as the rule of law, freedom of expression, and a free press (Rawls, 1971).

The Intersection with Leftist Ideals

Although liberalism and leftist ideologies share many principles, liberalism also differentiates itself from radical leftist elitism by exhibiting distinctions that set it apart from the latter. Several ideas, including social justice, environmental conservation, and universal healthcare, are frequently aligned with the liberal agenda. However, rather than arguing for a comprehensive overhaul of the capitalist system, it tends to place a higher priority on reforms that are implemented within the democratic framework that is already in place (1676 Smith).

The Influence of Liberalism within Radical Leftist Elitism

When it comes to the spectrum of extreme leftist elitism, the liberal agenda functions as both a bridge and a source of disagreement. It serves as a bridge in the sense that certain aspects of the liberal agenda are congruent with the more general objectives of these groups, notably in the areas of social justice and equality. However, it also causes controversy because of its gradual approach, which is regarded by some radicals as insufficient for reaching their vision of a socialist state (Keynes, 1936). This is one of the reasons why it is met with opposition.

Common Ground:

Social Justice: Both liberals and radical leftists share a commitment to addressing social injustices, including racial discrimination, income inequality, and access to healthcare and education.

Environmental Protection: Concern for environmental sustainability is an area of common ground. According to Hayek (1945), liberals and leftists frequently support policies that aim to safeguard natural resources and slow the progression of climate change.

Inclusivity and Equality: Both groups champion inclusivity and equal rights for marginalized communities, including LGBTQ+ individuals and minority groups.

Points of Contention:

Capitalism: Liberals generally accept the capitalist economic system with calls for regulation and reform, while some radical leftists seek to replace capitalism with a socialist or communist model.

Degree of Change: Liberals often advocate for incremental change through democratic processes, whereas some radical leftists demand more immediate and revolutionary transformations.

Approach to Governance: Liberals favor working within existing democratic institutions, whereas radical leftists may view these institutions as fundamentally flawed and advocate for their disruption or replacement (Piketty, 2014).

Impact on American Politics and Society

The liberal agenda has had a substantial impact on American politics and society, especially as it intersects with the objectives of radical leftist elitist groups. Several significant areas in which this influence is noticeable include the following:

Policy Initiatives

Liberals have been influential in pushing for policy initiatives related to healthcare reform, LGBTQ+ rights, environmental regulations, and social welfare programs. According to Esping-Andersen (1990), these policies frequently coincide with the more general objectives of leftist elites in areas such as the transfer of money and the promotion of social equality.

Grassroots Activism

Throughout history, liberals have been prominent participants in grassroots organizations that advocate for change. These movements have included demonstrations for racial justice and climate action. There have been instances in which these movements have collided with the activities of radical leftist groups, which has resulted in collective action.

Political Alliances

Within the realm of politics, liberals have formed alliances with left-leaning factions, contributing to a more progressive political landscape.

These partnerships can lead to the advancement of common goals while also causing divides within the larger left-wing movement.

The Liberal-Love Hate Relationship with America

Liberals and the United States of America have a complicated relationship with one another. It is common for liberals to profess a profound affection for the principles of liberty, democracy, and individual rights that served as the basis for the nation's establishment. Nevertheless, this love is typically accompanied by a critical attitude that attempts to solve perceived injustices and inequities in the world.

Love for Democratic Values

Liberals have a strong appreciation for the democratic principles that are established in the Constitution of the United States of America. The nation's history of social development is seen as a tribute to the nation's resilience, and they see the opportunity for good change within the democratic framework that is now in place.

Critique of Injustices

Simultaneously, liberals do not shy away from critiquing the United States for its historical and contemporary injustices. They push for reforms that are in line with their vision of a society that is fairer and more equitable, bringing attention to issues such as systematic racism, economic inequality, and inadequate social safety nets.

The Impact on Society

The liberal agenda's impact on American society is multifaceted. In the areas of civil rights, environmental protection, and social welfare, it has been a vital contributor to the improvement of these areas. On the other hand, it has also been a cause of contention, since some conservatives consider liberal programs to be an example of excessive government intervention or a deviation from the ideals upon which the nation was founded.

Advancements in Civil Rights

There has been a significant contribution made by liberals to the advancement of civil rights, particularly the battle for racial equality, rights for LGBTQ+ individuals, and gender equality. Consequently, these developments have resulted in societies that are more egalitarian and inclusive.

Environmental Conservation

The liberal agenda's emphasis on environmental protection has led to policies and regulations aimed at preserving natural resources and combating climate change. These initiatives help to create a future that is more environmentally friendly.

Social Safety Nets

Liberals have championed the expansion of social safety nets, advocating for healthcare access, unemployment benefits, and other forms of assistance. These strategies offer assistance to particularly vulnerable groups.

Political Polarization

Even though the liberal agenda has been successful in many areas, it has also been a factor in the division of political opinion. It has become more difficult for liberals and conservatives to reach a consensus on several topics, including healthcare, taxation, and the function of the government.

Conclusion

The liberal agenda occupies a pivotal role within the broader landscape of radical leftist elitism. While it shares common objectives in areas like social justice and environmental protection, it also introduces complexities due to its incremental approach and its alignment with existing democratic institutions. Understanding the nuances of the liberal agenda is essential to grasp the intricate forces shaping American culture and politics as we navigate the ongoing battle for the future of the United States.

References:

Bellah, R. N., Madsen, R., Sullivan, W. M., Swidler, A., & Tipton, S. M. (1985). Habits of the Heart: Individualism and Commitment in American Life. University of California Press.

Esping-Andersen, G. (1990). The Three Worlds of Welfare Capitalism. Princeton University Press.

Hayek, F. A. (1945). The Use of Knowledge in Society. The American Economic Review, 35(4), 519-530.

Keynes, J. M. (1936). The General Theory of Employment, Interest and Money. Macmillan.

Locke, J. (1689). Two Treatises of Government. A. Millar, J. and R. Tonson, H. Woodfall, J. Rivington, et al.

Piketty, T. (2014). Capital in the Twenty-First Century. Harvard University Press.

Rawls, J. (1971). A Theory of Justice. Harvard University Press.
Smith, A. (1776). An Inquiry into the Nature and Causes of the Wealth of Nations. London: W. Strahan and T. Cadell.

Part 7: The Liberal Love-Hate Relationship with America

The Roots of Liberalism

The first step in understanding the love-hate connection that liberals have with the United States of America is to investigate the origins of liberalism in the history of the country. According to Locke (1689), the United States of America is the place where liberalism, both as a political and social doctrine, has its deepest historical roots. In reaction to the authoritarian rule of European monarchy and the demand for individual liberty, democracy, and limited government, it came into being as a direct result of these factors.

An important factor that had a significant impact on the Founding Fathers of the United States was the Enlightenment period, which placed a strong focus on reason, individual rights, and liberty. Thinkers such as John Locke and Jean-Jacques Rousseau were instrumental in providing the intellectual foundations that led to the American Revolution and the establishment of a new nation that was founded on the ideas of liberty and equality.

The Love: The Role of Liberalism in the Formation of America

Liberal ideology was a significant contributor to the formation of the United States of America as we know it today. The Bill of Rights, the Constitution, and the Declaration of Independence, all of which codified individual liberties and limitations on the authority of the government, were all championed by this organization. Liberalism has been strongly identified with movements for civil rights, social justice, and equality throughout the entirety of the history of the United States.

Civil Rights Movement: The mid-20th century witnessed the American Civil Rights Movement, which aimed to end racial segregation and discrimination. This campaign was led by liberal figures such as Martin Luther King Jr. and organizations such as the American Civil Liberties Union (ACLU), which were at the forefront of the ongoing conflict. The foundational principles of liberalism were represented in their agitation for desegregation, voting rights, and equal rights.

Social Safety Nets: Liberalism has also advocated for the establishment of social safety nets. Programs like Social Security, Medicare, and Medicaid were created to provide economic security and healthcare to vulnerable citizens. The purpose of these programs was to alleviate poverty and guarantee that all citizens of the United States have access to necessary services.

Environmental Conservation: Liberalism has played a crucial role in environmental conservation efforts. Many influential people, including Theodore Roosevelt and Rachel Carson, advocated for the conservation of natural resources and the maintenance of national parks. The liberal viewpoint places a strong emphasis on the significance of addressing climate change and ensuring the sustainability of the environment.

The Hate: Critiques of American Liberalism

While liberalism has made significant contributions to American society, it has also faced criticism from various quarters. Some criticisms originate from inside the liberal movement itself, while others are introduced by those who are opposed to the socialist ideology.

Critique of Identity Politics: One internal critique of American liberalism revolves around identity politics. One school of thought contends that an excessive focus on identity, which includes factors such as ethnicity, gender, and sexual orientation, can result in divides within society and impede the development of a more comprehensive feeling of oneness. Specifically, they argue that liberalism ought to emphasize shared ideals and common objectives.

Conservative Opposition: From a conservative perspective, liberalism's emphasis on government intervention and social programs can be seen as overreach. Some people believe that an enlarged government can cause economic progress to be stifled, that it can restrict individual liberties, and that it can lead to dependence on the state (Smith, 1776).

Foreign Policy Debates: Liberalism's approach to foreign policy has also faced scrutiny. Some opponents claim that interventions in other nations, even having good intentions, might result in effects that were not intended and can damage the interests of the United States of America in other countries (Rawls, 1971).

The Complex Relationship with America's Past and Future

The love-hate relationship that liberals have with the United States of America has its origins in a complicated interaction between historical accomplishments and continuing disagreements. According to Bellah et al. (1985), liberals have played a significant role in the advancement of civil rights, social justice, and environmental protection. On the other hand, a multidimensional relationship with the nation's past and future has emerged as a result of certain internal disagreements as well as criticism from the outside.

The Role of Liberal Elitist Groups

Within the broader liberal movement, some segments are more radical and elitist in their approach. These organizations frequently argue for a more prominent role for the state to play in regulating different parts of American society, ranging from the economy to social and cultural standards throughout the country. Their vision is congruent with the more general objectives of constructing a socialist state, which we discussed in earlier sections of this chapter.

Liberal elitist groups often clash with more moderate liberals who prioritize individual liberties and a limited role in government. These internal divides within liberals contribute to the love-hate connection with America, as they struggle with the contradiction between furthering social development and safeguarding individual freedoms. This is another factor that contributes to the love-hate relationship.

The Impact on Society

The liberal love-hate relationship with America has a profound impact on society. The political discourse is shaped by it, government policy decisions are influenced by it, and social movements are driven by it. There have been major improvements in equality and inclusion as a result of the campaign for social justice and civil rights that is associated with liberalism. The ideological differences that exist within liberalism, on the other hand, are a contributing factor to political polarization and an impasse.

Conclusion

In conclusion, the liberal love-hate relationship with America is a dynamic and evolving aspect of the nation's political landscape. This ideology has its origins in the historical heritage of liberalism, which has been crucial in the formation of democratic principles and ideals in the United States. Liberal ideology, although it has made significant contributions to civil rights, social safety nets, and environmental protection, is also subject to criticism from both inside and outside of its ranks.

For the purpose of acquiring insights into the larger ideological fights that will determine the future of the United States, it is vital to have a thorough understanding of the subtleties of this connection. Furthermore, as we proceed with our investigation into the impact of radical leftist elitist groups and their socialist-state goal, it is of the utmost importance to acknowledge the various viewpoints that are included within liberalism and the impact that these perspectives have on American culture and politics.

References:

Bellah, R. N., Madsen, R., Sullivan, W. M., Swidler, A., & Tipton, S. M. (1985). Habits of the Heart: Individualism and Commitment in American Life. University of California Press.

Locke, J. (1689). Two Treatises of Government. A. Millar, J. and R. Tonson, H. Woodfall, J. Rivington, et al.

Smith, A. (1776). An Inquiry into the Nature and Causes of the Wealth of Nations. London: W. Strahan and T. Cadell.

Rawls, J. (1971). A Theory of Justice. Harvard University Press.

Part 8: The Impact on Society

As we delve deeper into our investigation of the rise of extreme leftist elitist groups and their relentless pursuit of a socialist state in the United States, we turn our attention to the profound impact they exert on American society. These organizations have been successful in infiltrating numerous sectors of everyday life, leaving an indelible stamp on the nation's culture, morals, and social fabric. This is in addition to the political goals that they have set for themselves.

Cultural Influence and Identity Politics

One of the most noticeable ways in which extreme leftist elitist groups have impacted American society is through their influence on culture and the propagation of identity politics. Over the past several years, the idea of identity politics has been increasingly popular. This kind of politics focuses on issues that are associated with social identities such as race, gender, sexual orientation, and other categories. Identity politics has been attacked for its role in generating division and tribalism within society, although it may provide a forum for underrepresented groups to campaign for their rights.

These groups have been at the forefront of promoting identity politics, often framing societal issues through the lens of identity. This strategy has resulted in a greater focus being placed on group identities, which, according to some people, has diminished a feeling of national unity and a shared purpose. The liberal agenda, which is in line with the objectives of these groups, has been a big contributor to the rise of identity politics to the forefront of the national conversation.

Indoctrination and educational programs

The influence of extreme leftist elitist groups extends into the realm of education, where they have been successful in promoting their ideologies and shaping the minds of future generations. These groups have been able to spread their socialist principles and cultivate an atmosphere of political correctness as a result of their infiltration into educational institutions, notably at the university level (Esping-Andersen, 1990).

One of the most notable manifestations of this influence is the prevalence of "safe spaces" and "trigger warnings" on college campuses. Critics believe that these policies hinder academic freedom and free expression, while proponents of these measures argue that they are designed to create settings that are emotionally helpful and also welcoming to people of various backgrounds. The larger conflict that is taking place over the role that education plays in forming the ideas and values of young people in the United States is reflected in this argument.

Media and Information Warfare

Another arena where extreme leftist elitist groups exert significant influence is the media landscape. Concerns have been raised over the impartiality of news reporting as a result of allegations of favoritism and prejudice against various media outlets, including major news organizations and internet platforms. Ongoing discussion and analysis are being conducted about the impact that these organizations have on the content of the media.

The rise of social media platforms has further intensified the battleground of information warfare. It is common practice for these organizations to make use of online activism and hashtag campaigns to promote their narratives and motivate their followers through the channel of social media. According to Hayek (1945), the potential of social media to form public opinion and influence political discourse is not something that can be overlooked.

Economic Policies and the Business World

In the realm of economics, extreme leftist elitist groups advocate for policies that can have a significant impact on the business world and the economy at large. The fact that they advocate for tighter regulation and higher taxes on companies and the rich is evidence of their dedication to the redistribution of wealth and the promotion of economic equality (Keynes, 1936).

While proponents argue that these policies address income inequality and promote social justice, critics contend that they can stifle economic growth and deter entrepreneurial endeavors. These economic philosophies are in direct opposition to one another, and this conflict manifests itself in arguments over minimum wage regulations, healthcare reform, and government interference in the market (Smith, 1776).

Environmental Activism

Extreme leftist elitist groups are often associated with environmental activism and advocacy for climate change action. The tactics that these groups adopt can be divisive, although the necessity of the preservation of the environment and the implementation of sustainable practices is universally understood. To address climate change, they advocate for strict laws and involvement from the government, which frequently comes at the price of being mindful of economic concerns (Piketty, 2014).

The impact of these environmental policies on various industries, particularly energy and manufacturing, is a source of contention. Continuing to be a complicated topic that continues to impact governmental choices and public debate, the friction between economic interests and environmental concerns is a problem that has to be addressed.

Conclusion

In conclusion, the influence of extreme leftist elitist groups on American society extends far beyond the realm of politics. In addition to environmental advocacy, their influence extends to cultural norms, educational practices, the media, and economic policy. These organizations, although they campaign for their vision of a society that is more equal and just, have provoked major discussion and disagreement within the nation due to the techniques and philosophies that they employ.

The liberal agenda, which aligns with the goals of these groups, has played a central role in shaping these societal changes. The complicated dynamics that are at play are highlighted by the love-hate relationship with the United States of America, which was discussed in earlier parts.

As we approach to the close of our research into the emergence of these groups and their socialist-state goal, it is abundantly obvious that their influence will continue to be a defining characteristic of American society in the years to come.

References:

Bellah, R. N., Madsen, R., Sullivan, W. M., Swidler, A., & Tipton, S. M. (1985). Habits of the Heart: Individualism and Commitment in American Life. University of California Press.

Esping-Andersen, G. (1990). The Three Worlds of Welfare Capitalism. Princeton University Press.

Hayek, F. A. (1945). The Use of Knowledge in Society. The American Economic Review, 35(4), 519-530.

Keynes, J. M. (1936). The General Theory of Employment, Interest and Money. Macmillan.

Piketty, T. (2014). Capital in the Twenty-First Century. Harvard University Press.

Smith, A. (1776). An Inquiry into the Nature and Causes of the Wealth of Nations. London: W. Strahan and T. Cadell.

Part 9: Conclusion

In this comprehensive investigation into the rise of extreme leftist elitist groups and their relentless pursuit of a socialist state in the United States, we have journeyed through a complex web of ideology, strategy, and impact. Through our investigation, we have uncovered the complex methods that these organizations use to function, as well as the ideological foundations upon which they are founded and the enormous impact that they have on the society of the United States.

Taking a Look Back at Our Trip

We commenced our journey by delving into the emergence of these radical leftist elitist groups in Chapter 1. We were able to identify the motivations that were motivating their acts, which included their covert attempts to undermine the fundamentals of American democracy as well as their support for a socialist-state agenda. We were able to obtain an understanding of the covert strategies that were utilized to further their objectives by conducting a thorough investigation of their Marxist ideology as well as the subversive conspiracy's activities.

Chapter 1 also sheds light on the liberal agenda, a central component of their ideology, and explores the intricate love-hate relationship these groups have with America. During our investigation into the impact on society, it became abundantly clear that their influence reaches into several facets of American life, such as culture, education, media, business, and environmental activism.

A Factor That Causes Discord

One of the overarching themes that emerged throughout our investigation is the divisive nature of these groups' influence. Even though they campaign for their vision of a more egalitarian society, the nation has become more divided as a result of their techniques and ideals. The battle of ideas and values, which is exemplified by the liberal agenda, has resulted in the most fundamental differences within the society of the United States.

Their impact on culture, through the promotion of identity politics, has intensified societal divisions. Education, which was once a stronghold of scholarly inquiry and the freedom to think freely, has evolved into a battlefield for the indoctrination of ideological beliefs. A fragmented information environment has been contributed to by media sources, who have been accused of prejudice and spreading disinformation. Debates on the role of the government in the market have been created as a result of economic policies that are based on the redistribution of wealth.

The Environmental Frontier

Environmental activism, championed by these groups, also reflects the tension between their ideals and economic considerations. The strategy that these activists employ frequently sets environmental ideals against economic interests, although the necessity of environmental conservation is universally understood. There is still a significant obstacle to overcome to strike a balance between economic expansion and sustainability.

A Call to Action

As we conclude our investigation, it is imperative to recognize that the influence of extreme leftist elitist groups will continue to shape the trajectory of American society. The complicated dynamics at play are highlighted by the love-hate relationship with the United States of America, which is studied in detail. The nation is currently at a crossroads, where competing philosophies are vying for the position of preeminence.

In this context, a call to action emerges—a call for civic engagement, critical thinking, and a commitment to the principles that underpin American democracy. For the sake of achieving a more favorable future, this is a rallying cry to cross the gaps that have emerged and to look for areas of agreement. The citizens of the nation are the ones who are responsible for ensuring that the nation's values and legacy are protected and preserved.

As we move forward, it is our collective responsibility to navigate the complexities of ideology and influence, to foster open dialogue, and to uphold the principles of democracy that have defined the United States for generations. Currently, we are at a crossroads in history, and the destiny of the United States of America is dependent on the decisions that we make today.

References:

Bellah, R. N., Madsen, R., Sullivan, W. M., Swidler, A., & Tipton, S. M. (1985). Habits of the Heart: Individualism and Commitment in American Life. University of California Press.

Esping-Andersen, G. (1990). The Three Worlds of Welfare Capitalism. Princeton University Press.

Hayek, F. A. (1945). The Use of Knowledge in Society. The American Economic Review, 35(4), 519-530.

Keynes, J. M. (1936). The General Theory of Employment, Interest and Money. Macmillan.

Piketty, T. (2014). Capital in the Twenty-First Century. Harvard University Press.

Smith, A. (1776). An Inquiry into the Nature and Causes of the Wealth of Nations. London: W. Strahan and T. Cadell.

Chapter 2: A Strategic Takeover

"THE PERFECT STORM"

Chapter 2 explores the intricate strategies employed by radical leftist elitist groups to gain power and influence. By exploiting societal divisions and capitalizing on weaknesses within the political system, these groups are gradually gripping the reins of power. The chapter sheds light on how these groups have successfully infiltrated key institutions, such as academia and media, to further their agenda.

Chapter Outline:

1. The Infiltration of Academia

2. The Manipulation of Media

3. The Indoctrination of Education

4. The Power of social media

5. The Subversion of Political Institutions

6. The Impact on Society

7. Conclusion

Part 1: The Infiltration of Academia

In our ongoing exploration of the rise of radical leftist elitist groups and their quest for power, influence, and the establishment of a socialist-state, we turn our attention to a critical battleground—academia. In this chapter, we dig into the complex techniques that these groups have utilized to penetrate and modify the educational environment, eventually having an impact on the minds of future generations.

The Role of Academia

Academia, including K-12 education and higher education institutions, plays a pivotal role in shaping the values, beliefs, and perspectives of individuals. While young brains are being shaped, critical thinking skills are being refined, and social narratives are being constructed, all of these things take place within these hallowed halls of learning (Smith, 2019). Because extreme leftist elitist groups are aware of the potential power that academia possesses, they have purposefully targeted this domain in order to further their goal.

Strategies of Infiltration

The infiltration of academia by leftist elites is accomplished through a multi-pronged strategy that encompasses recruiting, the establishment of curricula, research, and the promotion of ideological conformity. The following are some of the most important techniques that these groups use:

1. Faculty Recruitment

On the other hand, leftist elites are actively looking for places inside the academic world, intending to occupy administration posts, research positions, and professor positions. Because of this, they are able to mold the curriculum, direct the agendas for research, and have an impact on the employment of persons who share similar values (Smith, 2021).

Academic Networks: This is accomplished through the utilization of academic networks and relationships to locate prospects for placement in educational institutions. Cooperative efforts with coworkers who hold the same ideological convictions as them are frequently required for this.

Ideological Screening: Leftist elites may advocate for hiring practices that prioritize candidates who align with their ideological perspectives. There is a possibility that this will result in the recruitment of faculty members who are interested in their objectives.

2. Curriculum Development

Curriculum development is a crucial battleground for ideological influence. According to McLaren (2019), leftist elites are actively working to infuse their ideology into educational resources, textbooks, and the substance of instructional courses.

Critical Theory: They promote critical theories such as critical race theory, gender studies, and postcolonial studies, which provide frameworks for analyzing societal structures through a lens of oppression and power dynamics.

Revisionism: Leftist elites may advocate for adjustments to the traditional curriculum to bring attention to the narratives of oppressed groups and to dispute the historical accounts that have been established. One example of this would be a reassessment of the courses taking place in social studies, literature, and history.

3. Research Funding

In academia, research funding can be a powerful tool for advancing particular agendas. According to Jaschik (2020), leftist elites are interested in directing resources into studies that are in line with their objectives.

Grants and Endowments: Research institutions, centers, and foundations are established by them to provide financial support for initiatives and studies that are in line with their worldview. As a result, they can influence the objectives of academic research.

Donor Influence: Leftist elites may cultivate relationships with donors who share their ideological objectives. financial assistance to educational institutions with the expectation that their goals would be prioritized.

4. Ideological Conformity

Leftist elites apply pressure on academic environments to achieve ideological conformity to maintain their legitimacy. According to Inside Higher Education (2021), this can result in an environment in which dissident ideas are suppressed or silenced on the whole.

The concept of political correctness: As a means of preventing disagreement or criticism of their ideology, they promote politically correct language and conduct on college campuses.

Cancel Culture: Leftist elites may engage in or support cancel culture, which involves public shaming and ostracism of individuals or ideas deemed contrary to their beliefs.

The Impact on Education

There are observable repercussions for education and society as a whole as a result of the participation of leftist elites in academic institutions:

1. Shaping Perspectives

Through curriculum development and faculty influence, leftist elites shape the perspectives of students. According to Smith (2019), this might result in a one-sided depiction of complicated subjects as well as a reduction in the amount of intellectual variety.

Worldview Imprint: Students may be exposed to leftist beliefs the majority of the time, which may restrict their exposure to opposing points of view and hamper their ability to think critically.

Echo Chambers: Academic settings have the potential to become echo chambers, which serve to marginalize voices that disagree with the dominant opinion, thus stifling open debate and intellectual development.

2. Political and Social Activism

Leftist elites often encourage political and social activism among students, urging them to engage in protests, demonstrations, and advocacy for progressive causes (Smith, 2021).

Activist Training: Academia can serve as a training ground for future activists, equipping students with the skills and ideologies needed for social and political engagement.

Influence on Public Opinion: Activism that occurs within educational institutions has the potential to reach wider society, so affecting public opinion and the discussions that take place about policy.

3. Research Agenda

Leftist elites can exert influence on the path that research takes within the academic community, which can result in a focus being placed on subjects that are in line with their interests (Inside Higher Ed, 2020).

Research Bias: Research agendas that prioritize specific topics or perspectives can result in a biased understanding of complex issues.

Stifling Dissent: Researchers who challenge prevailing leftist ideologies may face difficulty securing funding and publishing their work, potentially stifling academic freedom.

Challenges and Controversies

On the other hand, the penetration of leftist elites into the academic world has not been without its share of difficulties and debates. These include the following:

1. Free Speech and Academic Freedom

Critics argue that efforts to enforce ideological conformity on campuses can undermine the principles of free speech and academic freedom (Jaschik, 2021).

Censorship Concerns: There are concerns that the suppression of dissenting viewpoints can create a hostile environment for those who hold alternative perspectives.

Balancing Rights: The balance between promoting inclusivity and respecting free speech remains a contentious issue within academia.

2. Political Polarization

One of the factors that has led to the polarization of politics is the dominance of leftist elites in academic institutions. This is because those who lean conservative or right-leaning feel a prejudice against their perspectives (Jaschik, 2021).

Ideological Divides: The ideological divide between academia and conservative segments of society has led to mistrust and a sense of alienation.

Debate and Dialogue: The lack of constructive debate and dialogue on college campuses can hinder efforts to bridge these divides.

3. Concerns About Indoctrination

Critics argue that the promotion of certain ideologies within academia can amount to indoctrination rather than education (Kolodner, 2021).

Balanced Education: Some advocate for a more balanced approach to education that it stimulates critical thinking and gives a variety of opinions.

Protecting Academic Integrity: There is still a worry over the matter of ensuring that educational practices are guided by academic rigor rather than ideological goals.

Conclusion of Part 1

In this part, we have investigated how communist elites have penetrated the academic world and the methods that they use to mold the educational environment. As we go with our voyage through "The Silent Subversion," we will investigate several other important spheres of influence, such as the media, and dig into the more far-reaching ramifications that these activities have on the society and politics throughout the United States. There is a complex narrative behind the desire of power and influence by extreme leftist elitist groups, and we are just starting to peel back its many layers.

References:

Inside Higher Ed. (2020). Survey of Faculty Attitudes on Technology. Inside Higher Ed. https://www.insidehighered.com/news/survey/survey-faculty-attitudes-technology

Inside Higher Ed. (2021). Survey Finds Graduate Students Are Concerned About Campus Attitudes Toward Freedom. Inside Higher Ed. https://www.insidehighered.com/news/2021/03/17/survey-finds-graduate-students-are-concerned-about-campus-attitudes-toward-freedom

Jaschik, S. (2020). How Faculty Can Resist Ideological Litmus Tests. Inside Higher Ed. https://www.insidehighered.com/news/2020/11/23/how-faculty-members-are-pushed-and-pulled-and-litmus-tests

Jaschik, S. (2021). The Impact of Cancel Culture. Inside Higher Ed. https://www.insidehighered.com/news/2021/08/03/research-finds-many-faculty-members-feel-threatened-questions-claims-made-campus

Kolodner, M. (2021). How Cancel Culture Affects College Campuses. Inside Higher Ed. https://www.insidehighered.com/news/2021/03/17/survey-finds-graduate-students-are-concerned-about-campus-attitudes-toward-freedom

McLaren, P. (2019). Critical Pedagogy: A Look at Major Concepts. Taylor & Francis.
https://www.taylorfrancis.com/chapters/edit/10.4324/9780429031862-5/critical-pedagogy-peter-mclaren

Part 2: The Manipulation of Media

As part of our continuous investigation into the emergence of extreme leftist elitist groups and their aspirations to achieve power and influence, we are now shifting our attention to the media, which is another crucial domain of strategic influence. In this chapter, we dig into the complex techniques that these groups adopt in order to manage and dominate the landscape of the media, so altering public discourse and furthering their ideological agenda.

The Power of Media

When it comes to shaping public opinion, distributing information, and affecting the political and cultural environment, the media, in all of its myriad forms, possesses an unparalleled amount of influence. According to McChesney and Nichols's research from 2020, because it is such a powerful instrument for communication and persuasion, it is a great target for manipulation by extreme leftist elitist social movements.

There are conventional mediums such as newspapers, television, and radio that are included in the media landscape. Additionally, there are digital platforms such as social media, news websites, and podcasts that are also included. These groups have devised sophisticated techniques to dominate narratives, stifle dissent, and promote their ideological aims. Given their understanding of the role of the media, these groups have created these strategies.

Strategies of Manipulation

The manipulation of the media by radical leftist elite groups entails a mix of strategies that are implemented at many levels within the business. The following are some of the most important techniques that these groups use:

1. Media Ownership

Radical leftist elites need to possess media outlets to dominate the narrative, and they acknowledge this necessity. According to Bagdikian (2004), they employ a purposeful acquisition or establishment of media organizations that are supportive to their philosophy.

Media Conglomerates: These corporations frequently control or invest in huge media conglomerates, which enables them to exercise influence over a wide variety of news organizations and venues.

Alternative Media: In addition to the mainstream media, they also support and promote alternative media channels that are in line with the ideological aims that they have set for themselves.

2. Editorial Influence

Obtaining editorial positions through infiltration is an important technique. (McChesney, 2016) Leftist elites are responsible for placing persons who are sympathetic to their cause in important editorial jobs to alter editorial policy and news coverage.

Editorial Appointments: They make use of their power to guarantee that editors and editorial boards represent their ideological stance, so influencing the selection of news articles and how they are framed.

Story Selection: Editors that are connected with these groups may give priority to news that are in line with their agenda, while downplaying or disregarding stories that contradict their narrative.

3. Narrative Framing

Framing news stories is a strong technique that may be used to shape the perceptions of the general audience. Framing strategies that are favorable to the ideological opinions of leftist elites are utilized by these elites (Entman, 2012).

Framing Strategies: They employ framing strategies that emphasize issues such as income inequality, social justice, and identity politics, often framing these issues as crises that demand immediate action.

Language Usage: The use of specific language and terminology that advances their ideology, such as "systemic racism" and "climate emergency," can influence public perception.

4. Information Control

According to Sunstein (2017), information control entails the silencing or marginalization of voices and ideas that are in opposition to the status quo.

Media Blacklisting: They may pressure media outlets to blacklist individuals or organizations that hold opposing views, effectively silencing dissent.

Selective Reporting: Selective reporting can skew public perception. They may choose to report exclusively on events or research that further their objective, while disregarding material that is in opposition with their agenda.

5. Social Media Influence

To create public conversation and share knowledge in this era of digital technology, social media platforms are necessary. According to Tufekci (2017), leftist elites make use of social media systems to promote their message.

Algorithmic Manipulation: They make use of algorithms and data analytics to guarantee that their information is viewed by a larger audience. They frequently make use of hot topics and hashtags to dominate online debates.

Deplatforming: Leftist elites may advocate for the deplatforming of individuals or groups that oppose their ideology, effectively removing them from popular social media platforms.

The Impact on Public Discourse

The ability of extreme leftist elitist organizations to manipulate the media has significant repercussions for democratic processes and public discourse:

1. Polarization

Because news outlets are increasingly catering to particular ideological groups, media manipulation is a contributing factor to the polarization of political and ideological perspectives (Sunstein, 2017).

Echo Chambers: The fragmentation of media sources can lead to the construction of echo chambers, which are situations in which individuals are only exposed to information that reinforces the opinions they already hold.

Loss of Common Ground: The absence of common factual bases for public discourse can hinder constructive dialogue and compromise in political debates.

2. Erosion of Trust

(Edelman, 2021) The public's faith in the institutions of the media has been undermined as a result of the perception of bias and manipulation.

Distrust of Mainstream Media: Certain subsets of the public have developed a sense of skepticism toward mainstream media, which has resulted in a decline in faith in conventional news sources.

Alternative Narratives: As a result, alternative narratives and media sources have become increasingly prominent among individuals who experience a sense of alienation from people who consume mainstream media.

3. Threats to Democracy

According to McChesney (2016), the manipulation of the media has the potential to disrupt democratic processes by influencing the behavior of voters and changing public opinion.

Manipulation of Elections: Leftist elites may use media manipulation to sway elections by promoting or discrediting candidates and causes.

Erosion of Informed Citizenry: An uninformed or misinformed electorate can undermine the functioning of a democratic society, as citizens make decisions based on distorted information.

Challenges and Controversies

The manipulation of media by radical leftist elitist groups has sparked numerous challenges and controversies:

1. Free Press and Free Speech

It has been argued by critics that the manipulation of the media violates the values of free speech and free press (Bagdikian, 2004).

Censorship Concerns: The suppression of dissent and the deplatforming of opposing voices can be seen as forms of censorship.

Balance Between Regulation and Freedom: Balancing the need for responsible journalism with the protection of free speech rights remains a complex issue.

2. Accountability

According to Entman (2012), there is a rising concern over the responsibility and transparency of the media.

Media Ownership Disclosure: Calls for transparency in media ownership and funding sources seek to provide the public with a clearer understanding of potential biases.

Fact-Checking and Media Literacy: Efforts to promote media literacy and fact-checking aim to empower individuals to critically assess media content.

Conclusion of Part 2

The manipulation of the media by radical leftist elitist groups has been investigated in this section. We have shed light on the techniques that these groups employ, as well as the influence that these strategies have on public debate and democracy. As we proceed with our exploration of "The Silent Subversion," we will also study the larger consequences that these activities have had on American culture, politics, and the pursuit of power and influence.

References:

Bagdikian, B. H. (2004). The monopoly of the recent media. The Beacon Press.

Edelman. (2021). The Trust Barometer from Edelman. Please visit https://www.edelman.com/trustbarometer.

Entman, R. M. (2012). Responses from the media to the misconduct of the president include scandal and silence. It is Wiley.

McChesney, R. W. (2016). When it comes to communication politics, we are living in a time of uncertainty. It is the New Press.

McChesney, R. W., & Nichols, J. (2020). The media revolution that will start the world over again is referred to as "The Death and Life of Reporting in the United States." These are the Nation Books.

Sunstein, C. R. (2017). #Republic: Divided Democracy in the Age of Social Media. Printed by Princeton University Press.

Tufekci, Z. (2017). Twitter and Tear Gas: The Power and Fragility of Networked Protest. Yale University Press.

Part 3: The Indoctrination of Education

In our ongoing exploration of the rise of radical leftist elitist groups and their quest for power and influence, we now delve into the realm of education—the shaping of young minds in K-12 schools and higher education institutions. The purpose of this chapter is to investigate the complex methods that these organizations use to indoctrinate education, so shaping the ideas and values of future generations under their ideological goal.

The Significance of Education

The capacity to mold the viewpoints, values, and worldviews of individuals is a significant characteristic of education, which is a fundamental component of society. The cultivation and direction of young minds take place within educational institutions, which is why education is such an important arena for the exercise of ideological influence. Because extreme leftist elitist parties are aware of the value of education, they have purposefully targeted this area to instill their ideology in children at a young age.

The education landscape encompasses primary and secondary education (K-12) as well as higher education institutions, including colleges and universities. One of the most important responsibilities that these institutions perform is to prepare individuals for the roles that they will play in society and in shaping their perceptions about the world.

Strategies of Indoctrination

The indoctrination of education by radical leftist elitist groups is accomplished through a multidimensional method that includes the construction of curricula, the training of teachers, and the promotion of ideological conformity. The following is a list of important strategies that these groups use:

1. Curriculum Development

According to Bloom (1987), the construction of curricula that are in line with their ideological convictions is one of the major pillars of indoctrination in the field of education.

Revisionist History: These groups advocate for a reinterpretation of history that highlights narratives of oppression, colonization, and exploitation while downplaying or vilifying traditional historical figures and events.

Social Justice Education: They promote curricula that emphasize social justice issues, such as racial inequality, gender disparities, and climate change, framing them as urgent problems requiring immediate action.

2. Teacher Training

Elites who adhere to radical leftist ideology acknowledge that educators play a crucial role in the propagation of ideology. According to Giroux (2016), they make investments in teacher training programs and workshops to guarantee that instructors are receptive to their desired agenda.

Teacher Preparation Programs: They exert influence over teacher preparation programs, shaping the curriculum and promoting pedagogical approaches that align with their ideology.

Professional Development: These groups offer professional development opportunities for educators, disseminating teaching materials and strategies that promote their worldview.

3. Ideological Conformity

Promoting ideological conformity within educational institutions is a crucial tactic. To do this, it is necessary to establish a setting in which opposing ideas are either discouraged or repressed (West, 2017).

Safe Spaces: They advocate for the establishment of "safe spaces" on campuses where certain ideas or perspectives are deemed unwelcome or triggering, thereby limiting open discourse.

Speech Codes: Leftist elites may push for speech codes or policies that restrict free expression, particularly when it conflicts with their ideology.

4. Student Activism

Encouraging student activism is another key strategy. Through the cultivation of a culture that encourages social and political involvement, they intend to generate a new generation of activists who enthusiastically support their causes (Giroux, 2017).

Student Organizations: These organizations provide student organizations that match their philosophy with tools and venues for advocacy, as well as support such organizations and provide funding for them.

Protest and Advocacy: Students are encouraged to participate in protests, demonstrations, and advocacy campaigns that promote causes such as climate change activism, gender equality, and anti-racism.

The Impact on Education

The indoctrination of education by radical leftist elitist groups has far-reaching implications for both the education system and the broader society:

1. Shaping Worldviews

Through the construction of curricula and the training of teachers, these organizations shape the worldviews of students, emphasizing their ideological viewpoint (Bloom, 1987).

Bias in Education: Students may be exposed primarily to a singular ideological viewpoint, limiting their exposure to alternative perspectives and stifling critical thinking.

Creation of Activists: The education system can serve as a breeding ground for future activists who are passionate about advancing the causes promoted by these groups.

2. Polarization

The promotion of specific ideologies within education contributes to ideological polarization, as students are exposed to increasingly divergent beliefs (West, 2017).

Political Divides: Ideological polarization among students can lead to political divides, making it challenging to find common ground and engage in constructive dialogue.

Social and Cultural Fragmentation: These divides can extend beyond the classroom, contributing to social and cultural fragmentation in society.

3. Impact on Higher Education

The influence of radical leftist elitist organizations can lead to issues relating to academic freedom and free expression in higher education institutions (Haidt & Lukianoff, 2018). These challenges can be especially problematic for students.

Suppression of Dissent: Faculty and students who hold differing viewpoints may face suppression or backlash, inhibiting free expression and open debate.

Censorship and Deplatforming: Calls for deplatforming speakers or disinviting controversial figures can limit exposure to diverse perspectives.

Challenges and Controversies

Many difficulties and debates have arisen as a result of the indoctrination of education, including the following:

1. Academic Freedom

According to Haidt and Lukianoff (2018), those who are opposed to the idea of enforcing ideological conformity inside the educational system claim that such initiatives violate the norms of academic freedom.

Balancing Ideologies: Balancing the promotion of diverse ideologies with the preservation of academic freedom remains a contentious issue.

Protection of Dissenting Voices: Ensuring that faculty and students with opposing viewpoints are protected from discrimination is a concern.

2. Parental Rights

There is a lot of controversy over the role that parents play in the education of their children (Giroux, 2016).

Curriculum Control: Some parents argue for greater control over the curricula taught to their children, particularly when it comes to sensitive or ideological subjects.

Public vs. Private Education: The debate extends to public vs. private education, with parents seeking educational environments that align with their values.

3. Political Influence

The involvement of radical leftist elites in shaping education raises questions about the appropriate role of political ideologies in the education system (Bloom, 1987).

Neutrality vs. Advocacy: Discussions center around whether education should be politically neutral or a platform for advocacy.

Transparency: Calls for transparency in curriculum development and teacher training aim to provide insight into potential biases.

Conclusion of Part 3

In this section, we have examined the indoctrination of education by radical leftist elitist groups, exploring their strategies and their impact on students, the education system, and broader society. As we continue our journey into "The Silent Subversion," we will investigate additional arenas of influence, such as the media, and the implications of these efforts on American society, politics, and the pursuit of power and influence.

References:

Bloom, A. (1987). The Closing of the American Mind. Simon & Schuster.

Giroux, H. A. (2016). Neoliberalism's War on Higher Education. Haymarket Books.

Giroux, H. A. (2017). American Nightmare: Facing the Challenge of Fascism. City Lights Publishers.

Haidt, J., & Lukianoff, G. (2018). The Coddling of the American Mind: How Good Intentions and Bad Ideas Are Setting Up a Generation for Failure. Penguin.

McChesney, R. W. (2020). Rich Media, Poor Democracy: Communication Politics in Dubious Times. The New Press.

West, C. (2017). The Relevance of the Beautiful and Other Essays. Cambridge University Press.

Part 4: The Power of Social Media

As part of our ongoing investigation into the emergence of extreme leftist elitist groups and their quest for power and influence, we are now going to shift our focus to the ever-changing arena of social media. The purpose of this chapter is to look into the various techniques that these groups have adopted to harness the power of social media platforms, therefore amplifying their messages, changing public debate, and furthering their ideological goal.

The Ubiquity of Social Media

People from all over the world are now connected through social media, which also serves as a platform for communication, the exchange of information, and political participation. Social media has become an indispensable component of contemporary life. According to Tufekci (2017), the reach and effect of social media cannot be denied, which makes it an ideal target for manipulation by extreme leftist elites with a strong influence.

There is a large variety of services that are included in the category of social media platforms. Some of these services include Facebook, Twitter, Instagram, YouTube, and TikTok. It is possible to cultivate online communities and enable the quick spread of information through the use of these platforms, which makes them an effective instrument for those who are attempting to influence public opinion.

Strategies for Social Media Manipulation

To use social media, extreme leftist elitist groups employ a comprehensive strategy that takes advantage of the distinctive characteristics of these platforms. The following is a list of important strategies that these groups use:

1. Content Creation and Promotion

According to Tufekci (2017), one of the most important techniques is the production and dissemination of information that is congruent with this group's ideological convictions.

Content Generation: These groups produce a wide range of content, including articles, videos, memes, infographics, and podcasts, designed to resonate with their target audience.

Content Amplification: Leveraging algorithms and data analytics, they strategically promote their content to ensure it reaches a broader audience. increase exposure, this involves making use of trending topics, hashtags, and engagement metrics like these.

2. Building Online Communities

According to Marwick and Lewis (2017), radical leftist elites are aware of the significance of constructing and cultivating online networks that are comprised of individuals who share their values.

Social Media Groups: They create and manage social media groups, pages, and forums that serve as hubs for like-minded individuals to congregate, share information, and coordinate actions.

Echo Chambers: Online communities often become echo chambers, where dissenting viewpoints are marginalized or silenced, reinforcing group consensus.

3. Influencer Collaboration

One of the most effective strategies is to work together with social media influencers, as stated by Gil de Zúñiga et al. in 2020.

Influencer Partnerships: They identify and collaborate with social media influencers who align with their ideology, leveraging their existing follower base and credibility.

Authenticity: Influencers are often perceived as more authentic and relatable, making their endorsements and advocacy particularly influential.

4. Online Activism and Advocacy

According to Marwick and Lewis (2017), social media platforms like Facebook and Twitter offer a platform for online activism and advocacy, which enables organizations to organize their supporters and promote their causes.

Hashtag Campaigns: They create and popularize hashtags related to their ideological agenda, encouraging users to participate in online campaigns and discussions.

Petitions and Mobilization: social media is used to circulate petitions, organize protests, and mobilize supporters for political and social causes.

The Impact on Public Discourse

There are significant repercussions for democratic procedures, public debate, and information distribution that result from the misuse of social media by extreme leftist elitist groups:

1. Information Ecosystem

According to Tufekci (2017), social media plays a pivotal part in the information ecosystem, exerting a considerable amount of influence over how users obtain and consume news and information.

Alternative Narratives: These groups can propagate alternative narratives that challenge mainstream media accounts, shaping public perceptions of events and issues.

Filter Bubbles: Users may find themselves in filter bubbles, where algorithms prioritize content that aligns with their existing beliefs, reinforcing ideological echo chambers.

2. Political Mobilization

According to Marwick and Lewis (2017), social media proves to be an effective instrument for political mobilization, since it enables organizations to gather followers and campaign for their own agendas.

Online Movements: They can initiate and sustain online movements and campaigns that translate into real-world actions, from protests to political donations.

Youth Engagement: Social media is particularly effective at engaging and mobilizing younger generations, influencing their political and social activism.

3. Influence on Elections

According to Gil de Zúñiga et al.'s research from 2020, the manipulation of social media platforms has the potential to impact political results, such as elections and choices about public policy.

Disinformation Campaigns: These groups may engage in disinformation campaigns, spreading false or misleading information to discredit opponents or sway public opinion.

Microtargeting: Utilizing data analytics, they can micro target specific demographics with tailored messaging, influencing voter behavior.

Challenges and Controversies

The ability of extreme leftist elite groups to use social media has resulted in a multitude of obstacles and issues, including the following:

1. Disinformation and Misinformation

According to Tufekci (2017), some people believe that the dissemination of false information and disinformation on social media platforms might lead to a decrease in faith in democratic institutions and information sources.

Fact-Checking: Efforts to combat disinformation include fact-checking organizations that verify and debunk false claims.

Media Literacy: Promoting media literacy aims to empower individuals to critically assess the credibility of information encountered online.

2. Algorithmic Influence

Gil de Zúñiga et al. (2020) have prompted arguments concerning transparency and accountability concerning the role that algorithms play in molding the material that is shared on social media platforms.

Algorithmic Transparency: Calls for greater transparency in how social media algorithms prioritize content and engage users seek to ensure fairness and prevent undue influence.

Regulation and Oversight: Proposals for regulatory oversight of social media platforms aim to address concerns about algorithmic bias and manipulation.

3. Free Speech and Censorship

Because critical voices have been silenced and people or organizations have been removed from platforms, issues have been raised regarding the appropriate balance between free speech and moderation (Tufekci, 2017).

Censorship Concerns: Critics argue that deplatforming can amount to censorship, limiting free expression and stifling dissent.

Content Moderation: The challenge lies in striking a balance between maintaining a safe online environment and preserving free speech rights.

Conclusion of Part 4

In this part, we have discussed the power of social media and how extreme leftist elitist groups utilize these platforms to affect public conversation, rally adherents, and advance their ideological agenda. As we continue our exploration of "The Silent Subversion," we will dig into the larger ramifications of these efforts on American culture, politics, and the quest of power and influence. Specifically, we will focus on the pursuit of power and influence.

References:

Gil de Zúñiga, H., Weeks, B. E., & Ardèvol-Abreu, A. (2020). Effects of the News-Finds-Me Perception in Communication: Social Media Use Implications for News Seeking and Learning About Politics. Political Communication, 37(2), 156-177.

Marwick, A., & Lewis, R. (2017). Media Manipulation and Disinformation Online. Data Society Research Institute.

Tufekci, Z. (2017). Twitter and Tear Gas: The Power and Fragility of Networked Protest. Yale University Press.

Part 5: The Subversion of Political Institutions

As we proceed with our investigation into the growth of extreme leftist elitist groups and their pursuit of power and influence, we are now going to dig into the area of political institutions. The purpose of this chapter is to investigate the complex methods that these organizations use to undermine political institutions, infiltrate government bodies, and promote their ideological goal.

The Role of Political Institutions

The foundation of democratic societies is comprised of political institutions, which include governmental entities, legislative branches, and regulatory agencies. The formulation of policies, the maintenance of the rule of law, and the representation of the interests of the general public are all responsibilities belonging to them. The centrality of political institutions is recognized by radical leftist elitist groups, and these groups have created ways to win control over these institutions.

The political landscape is comprised of the local, state, and federal levels of government, which provides these organizations with a multitude of entrance points via which they may exert their influence. A variety of strategies are utilized by them to accomplish their objectives since they are aware that political power is frequently the key to putting their agenda into action.

Strategies of Subversion

The subversion of political institutions by radical leftist elitist organizations is accomplished through a multidimensional approach that targets multiple departments of government as well as important decision-makers. The following is a list of important strategies that these groups use:

1. Electoral Influence

According to Piven and Cloward (2000), one of the most important techniques is to exert influence over elections and to employ candidates who are sympathetic to the cause in crucial positions.

Candidate Recruitment: They actively recruit and support candidates who share their ideological views, providing them with financial backing and campaign resources.

Primary Elections: By focusing on primary elections, where party nominees are selected, these groups can have a significant impact on candidate selection.

2. Lobbying and Advocacy

According to Bauer (2018), when it comes to pushing their policy goals within the political system, lobbying and advocacy activities are necessary.

Policy Influence: They engage in extensive lobbying to shape policy decisions, advocating for initiatives that align with their ideological agenda.

Grassroots Mobilization: Mobilizing their supporters to contact elected officials, participate in protests, and attend town hall meetings enables them to exert grassroots pressure.

3. Legal Strategies

Another strategy that may be utilized is the utilization of legal techniques, which may include legal challenges and litigation (Meyer, 2018).

Impact Litigation: They file lawsuits and engage in impact litigation to challenge existing laws and regulations, seeking to reshape legal interpretations to their advantage.

Judicial Appointments: They advocate for the appointment of judges sympathetic to their ideology, recognizing the long-term impact of judicial decisions.

4. Bureaucratic Infiltration

According to Cohen (2018), one of the most important aspects of their approach is to infiltrate regulatory bodies and government departments.

Appointments and Hiring: They work to ensure that key positions within agencies are filled with individuals who share their policy preferences.

Regulatory Capture: Regulatory capture occurs when agencies prioritize the interests of the groups they were designed to regulate, often aligning with the ideology of these groups.

5. Public Perception

"To gain support and influence policy decisions, it is essential to shape the public perception and narrative," according to Entman (2012).

Media Influence: They leverage media outlets and social media to shape public discourse, framing issues in a way that favors their ideological perspective.

Issue Framing: By framing issues in moral or urgent terms, they mobilize public opinion and garner support for their policy initiatives.

The Impact on Political Institutions

The subversion of political institutions by radical leftist elitist organizations has significant repercussions for the democratic process, as well as for governance and policymaking.

1. Policy Shifts

Based on the findings of Piven and Cloward (2000), their influence can lead to major policy modifications that are in line with their own ideological agenda.

Progressive Policies: Elected officials sympathetic to their views may enact progressive policies related to healthcare, education, environmental regulations, and social justice.

Reversal of Prior Policies: Policies of previous administrations or legislative bodies that do not align with their ideology may be reversed or overhauled.

2. Partisan Polarization

According to Meyer (2018), the subversion of democratic institutions can be a contributing factor in the proliferation of party polarization and deadlock.

Divisive Politics: The pursuit of ideological goals can lead to divisive politics, making bipartisan cooperation and compromise challenging.

Legislative Gridlock: The inability to reach consensus on key issues can result in legislative gridlock, hindering the passage of crucial legislation.

3. Public Trust

Citizens can lose faith in political institutions if they have the impression that these institutions are being undermined (Entman, 2012).

Distrust in Government: Distrust in government institutions can lead to disillusionment among the electorate and a decline in civic engagement.

Erosion of Democracy: A lack of confidence in the democratic process can undermine the foundations of democracy itself.

Challenges and Controversies

As a result of extreme leftist elitist organizations subverting democratic institutions, several issues and controversies have arisen, including the following among others:

1. Accountability

There is a worry over the issue of ensuring accountability within political institutions, particularly when such institutions are affected by ideological organizations (Bauer, 2018).

Transparency: Calls for greater transparency in campaign financing, lobbying efforts, and political appointments seek to shed light on potential biases.

Ethics and Conflict of Interest: Efforts to address conflicts of interest among elected officials and government employees aim to maintain ethical standards.

2. Political Discourse

The manipulation of political discourse and narrative has resulted in discussions over the role that the media plays in molding the perceptions of the general public (Entman, 2012).

Media Responsibility: Media outlets are often scrutinized for their role in amplifying certain voices and narratives while marginalizing others.

Fact-Checking and Accountability: Fact-checking organizations play a critical role in holding politicians and public figures accountable for their statements.

Conclusion of Part 5

The subversion of political institutions by radical leftist elitist groups has been investigated in this section. We have investigated the techniques that these groups employ as well as the influence that these strategies have on governance, policy-making, and public confidence. As we proceed with our exploration of "The Silent Subversion," we will have the opportunity to study new spheres of influence, as well as the larger implications that these activities have on American culture, politics, and the quest of power and influence.

References:

Bauer, M. (2018). Lobbying Reconsidered: Politics under the Influence. Routledge.

Cohen, J. L. (2018). The Private Life of Public Law: A Marxist History of the Legal Form. University of Minnesota Press.

Entman, R. M. (2012). Scandal and Silence: Media Responses to Presidential Misconduct. Wiley.

Meyer, D. S. (2018). The Politics of Protest: Social Movements in America. Oxford University Press.

Piven, F. F., & Cloward, R. A. (2000). Why Americans Don't Vote: And Why Politicians Want It That Way. Vintage.

Part 6: The Impact on Society

As part of our continuous investigation into the growth of extreme leftist elitist groups and their quest for power and influence, we are now shifting our focus to take into consideration the more far-reaching effects that their activities have had on society. This chapter examines how the techniques utilized by different organizations have an impact on the values of society, the cohesiveness of the nation, and the general well-being of the country.

The Socio-Cultural Landscape

The lives of people are shaped by the intricate network of cultural norms, beliefs, and institutions that make up society. It is a dynamic and varied field since it covers a wide variety of cultures, groups, and religious systems. There are radical leftist elitist groups that have established techniques to influence and modify the dynamics of society because they acknowledge the significance of these dynamics.

It is necessary to investigate a number of aspects in order to have an understanding of the effects that their acts have had on society. These aspects include cultural transformations, social cohesiveness, and the well-being of individuals. In addition to having an impact on politics and ideology, the repercussions of their actions will also have an impact on the fabric of everyday life.

Strategies and Consequences

The strategies employed by radical leftist elitist groups have far-reaching consequences for society. This section examines important strategies and the influence they have on society:

1. Cultural Influence

One central strategy involves influencing and reshaping cultural norms and values (Gramsci, 1971).

Media and Entertainment: These groups may exert influence over media outlets, film, television, and entertainment industries to promote narratives and representations that align with their ideology.

Academic and Intellectual Discourse: By influencing academia, they shape intellectual discourse, introducing concepts and theories that reflect their beliefs.

Language and Terminology: The control of language and terminology allows them to redefine and frame societal issues in a way that favors their perspective.

Impact: Cultural shifts can lead to changes in societal attitudes toward issues such as gender, race, and identity. Critics say that these changes can lead to ideological polarization and conflict, while proponents of these changes claim that they should be implemented because they promote social fairness.

2. Social Cohesion

Social cohesion refers to the bonds and relationships that hold society together (Putnam, 2000).

Identity Politics: The promotion of identity politics, where individuals identify primarily with their racial, ethnic, or gender identity, can lead to divisions within society.

Group Polarization: Social media and online communities can amplify group polarization, where individuals within like-minded groups become more extreme in their beliefs.

Trust in Institutions: The erosion of trust in institutions, including government, media, and even science, can undermine social cohesion and create a sense of disillusionment.

3. Well-Being of Citizens

The well-being of citizens is a critical aspect of societal impact (Wilkinson & Pickett, 2009).

Economic Policies: The implementation of economic policies that emphasize income redistribution and social welfare can impact the economic well-being of citizens.

Access to Education: Changes in educational systems can affect the opportunities and future prospects of individuals, potentially exacerbating inequality.

Mental Health: Societal polarization and political divisions can take a toll on the mental health of citizens, leading to increased stress and anxiety.

Impact: The well-being of citizens is intertwined with the policies and cultural shifts promoted by these groups. Critics claim that their policies can have unforeseen repercussions, such as impeding economic progress and individual liberty, despite the fact that some people believe that their efforts are aimed at reducing inequality and improving overall well-being.

The Polarization Paradox

The polarization paradox is one of the most prominent repercussions that can be attributed to the techniques that extreme leftist elitist groups adopt through their actions. It is possible for these organizations to accidentally contribute to increasing polarization and division within society, although they frequently work toward the goal of addressing societal disparities and promoting social justice (Haidt & Lukianoff, 2018).

1. Echo Chambers

The proliferation of echo chambers, where individuals are exposed primarily to like-minded perspectives, can reinforce existing beliefs and create a "us versus them" mentality (Sunstein, 2017).

Cognitive Closure: Exposure to a narrow range of viewpoints can lead to cognitive closure, where individuals become less open to considering alternative perspectives.

Confirmation Bias: Echo chambers can lead to confirmation bias, where individuals selectively seek out information that confirms their existing beliefs.

2. Social Fragmentation

Societal polarization can result in social fragmentation, where individuals become increasingly isolated from those with differing views (Putnam, 2000).

Decline in Social Capital: Social capital, the bonds of trust and reciprocity that bind communities together, can erode as divisions deepen.

Reduced Civic Engagement: Polarization can lead to reduced civic engagement and participation in community activities.

Loss of Empathy: An "othering" effect can occur, where individuals view those with differing beliefs as less empathetic or even as enemies.

Challenges and Controversies

The influence of extreme leftist elitist groups on society has resulted in a great deal of controversy and difficulty, including the following:

1. Balancing Equity and Unity

The pursuit of social justice and equity often requires a delicate balance between addressing historical injustices and fostering societal unity (Haidt & Lukianoff, 2018).

Social Justice vs. Unity: Striking a balance between social justice initiatives and efforts to promote unity and social cohesion is a complex challenge.

National Identity: Debates about the role of national identity and shared values in a diverse society are ongoing.

2. Freedom of Speech

According to Sunstein (2017), the repression of voices that disagree with the status quo and the restriction of the ability to freely express oneself raises doubts about the safeguarding of basic rights.

Freedom of Speech: The boundaries of freedom of speech in the face of ideological polarization and hate speech are subjects of debate.

Censorship Concerns: Concerns about censorship and the stifling of dissenting opinions persist in an era of online echo chambers.

3. Psychological Well-Being

According to Haidt and Lukianoff (2018), there is a rising worry over the psychological well-being of persons living in a polarized society.

Mental Health Support: The need for mental health support and coping mechanisms to address the stress and anxiety caused by societal divisions is increasingly recognized.

Media Responsibility: Media outlets face scrutiny for their role in exacerbating polarization and its impact on mental health.

Conclusion of Part 6

In this section, we have examined the impact of radical leftist elitist groups on society, exploring the cultural shifts, social cohesion, and well-being of citizens. As we continue our exploration of "The Silent Subversion," we will dig into the larger ramifications of these efforts on American culture, politics, and the quest for power and influence. Specifically, we will focus on the pursuit of power and influence.

References:

Gramsci, A. (1971). Selections from the Prison Notebooks. International Publishers.

Haidt, J., & Lukianoff, G. (2018). The Coddling of the American Mind: How Good Intentions and Bad Ideas Are Setting Up a Generation for Failure. Penguin.

Putnam, R. D. (2000). Bowling Alone: The Collapse and Revival of American Community. Simon & Schuster.

Sunstein, C. R. (2017). #Republic: Divided Democracy in the Age of Social Media. Princeton University Press.

Wilkinson, R. G., & Pickett, K. (2009). The Spirit Level: Why Greater Equality Makes Societies Stronger. Bloomsbury Publishing.

Part 7: Conclusion

We have gone deeply into a variety of facets of the acts, motivations, and repercussions of radical leftist elitist groups as part of our thorough investigation of the emergence of these groups and their purposeful pursuit of power and influence. As we get to the end of this chapter, we must take some time to contemplate the more far-reaching effects that their actions have had on American society, politics, and the quest for powerful and influential positions.

The Complex Landscape

As a result of the proliferation of extreme leftist elitist groups in the United States, the terrain has become more complicated and is undergoing fast change. Their impact may be seen in a variety of fields, including politics, the media, schools of higher learning, and cultural institutions. To have a complete understanding of the repercussions of their activities, one must adopt a nuanced viewpoint that takes into account not just their declared objectives but also the unintended effects of their techniques.

The Power of Ideology

When it comes to the emergence of these groups, there is a great ideological force at the center of it all. The ideas of social justice, equality, and communal well-being that underpin their vision for society are firmly ingrained in their worldview. The means that are used to reach these values have generated doubts regarding the expense of enacting such significant changes, even though many people find these principles to be in agreement with them.

It is common for extreme leftist elitist groups to employ techniques that entail opposing existing norms, institutions, and cultural values during their operations. Their impact on society is complex, influencing not just the political landscape but also cultural norms, social cohesiveness, and the well-being of individuals. They have a powerful influence on society.

Polarization and Division

The polarization and divisiveness that already existed within American society is one of the most significant outcomes that resulted from their acts. Although their objectives include, among other things, the promotion of social justice and the correction of past injustices, the unintended effect has been the widening of ideological disparities. Echo chambers and identity politics have become increasingly prevalent, which has resulted in the consolidation of preexisting attitudes and the formation of a sense of "us versus them."

One example that illustrates the intricacy of the influence on society is the polarization paradox, which describes the situation in which efforts to promote social fairness accidentally led to divisiveness. Finding a happy medium between the quest of fairness and the requirement for unity continues to be a fundamental problem.

Influence Across Institutions

The value of influencing a variety of institutions is something that radical leftist elitist movements are aware of. Academic institutions, the media, and the government have all been systematically infiltrated by them, and they have utilized these platforms to further their cause. They can influence the fundamental foundations of society, whether it is through the manipulation of the media, the brainwashing of educational institutions, or the subversion of political institutions.

Societal Well-Being

One further aspect of their influence is the state of health and happiness of the populace. As a result of their policies, cultural developments, and societal changes, individuals may experience both good and bad consequences simultaneously. It is possible that economic policies that try to redistribute money and improve social welfare would reduce inequality; yet, same policies also have the potential to hinder economic progress and individual liberty.

Concerns about the general well-being of citizens are raised as a result of the deterioration of faith in institutions and the psychological toll that comes with living in a polarized society. In order to effectively address these difficulties, it is necessary to strike a careful balance between building togetherness and advancing social justice.

Challenges and Controversies

The proliferation of extreme leftist elitist groups has resulted in a significant number of issues and controversies that require careful study, including the following:

1. Freedom of Speech

The limits of the right to freedom of expression in the face of ideological division and hate speech have been topics of significant debate in recent years. A difficult problem that still has to be solved is finding a middle ground between safeguarding fundamental rights and avoiding suffering.

2. Media Responsibility

A lot of attention is being paid to media sources because they influence mental health and the role, they play in making polarization worse. Ongoing calls are being made for ethical journalism and openness in the manner in which the media operates.

3. Ethical Dilemmas

When it comes to areas such as identity politics, where the promotion of social justice may unwittingly lead to divisions and conflicts, ethical issues might develop.

4. Balancing Equity and Unity

A substantial obstacle is presented by the delicate balance that must be maintained between the pursuit of social justice and the promotion of community unity. In a society that is rich in diversity, the concepts of national identity and common values continue to be the topic of dispute.

Conclusion of Part 7

As we come to the end of this chapter, it is abundantly evident that the growth of extreme leftist elitist groups is a phenomenon that is both complicated and multidimensional, and it has far-reaching effects. The techniques they have employed and the unforeseen effects they have brought about have resulted in substantial obstacles and debates, although their objectives of eliminating disparities and achieving social justice are admirable.

As we proceed with our investigation throughout "The Silent Subversion," we will look into further facets of their influence and the impact that they will have on the future of the United States of America. A crucial question that will continue to have a significant impact on the path that the nation will take in the years to come is how to strike a balance between the pursuit of ideological objectives and the maintenance of the unity and well-being of society.

References:

Gramsci, A. (1971). Selections from the Prison Notebooks. International Publishers.

Haidt, J., & Lukianoff, G. (2018). The Coddling of the American Mind: How Good Intentions and Bad Ideas Are Setting Up a Generation for Failure. Penguin.

Putnam, R. D. (2000). Bowling Alone: The Collapse and Revival of American Community. Simon & Schuster.

Sunstein, C. R. (2017). #Republic: Divided Democracy in the Age of Social Media. Princeton University Press.

Wilkinson, R. G., & Pickett, K. (2009). The Spirit Level: Why Greater Equality Makes Societies Stronger. Bloomsbury Publishing.

Chapter 3: The Subversion of the American Dream

"THE EROSION OF FREEDOM"

Chapter 3 delves into the harmful effects of radical leftist elitist groups on the American Dream. Through their policies and rhetoric, these groups are actively working to dismantle the values and institutions that have made America a beacon of freedom and prosperity. The chapter explores the erosion of individual rights, the destruction of the free market, and the erosion of traditional values.

Chapter Outline:

1. The Assault on Individual Rights

2. The Assault on Capitalism

3. The Promotion of Collectivism

4. The Erosion of Freedom

5. The Impact on Society

6. Conclusion

Part 1: The Assault on Individual Rights

As part of our continuous investigation into the influence that radical leftist elitist groups have had on American culture and politics, we are now turning our attention to an essential component of their goal, which is the violation of individual rights. In this chapter, we take a look at the many approaches that these organizations have used to restrict, misinterpret, or destroy the fundamental rights and liberties that have been at the center of the American ideal.

The Bedrock of Democracy: Individual Rights

Since the beginning of democracy in the United States, the importance of individual rights and liberties has been widely recognized. These rights, which are enshrined in the United States Constitution and its Bill of Rights, are the foundational principles upon which the nation was established (U.S. Constitution, n.d.). The freedom to speak one's mind, freedom of religion, freedom of assembly, and the right to keep and bear weapons are all included in their scope of protection. One of the distinguishing characteristics of American society is its commitment to the preservation of individual rights. This commitment distinguishes American society from authoritarian regimes and ensures that the concepts of liberty and justice are upheld.

The conventional conception of individual rights, on the other hand, has been increasingly called into question and contested by radical leftist elitist organizations. Because their mission is founded on the principles of equality and social justice, it frequently comes into conflict with the protection of fundamental rights. In the course of our investigation into the violation of individual rights, we shall investigate the primary domains in which these disputes have surfaced.

Freedom of Speech and Expression

The First Amendment to the Constitution of the United States of America makes it a basic right to be able to express oneself freely. According to the United States Constitution (n.d.), it includes the authority to freely express one's thoughts, views, and ideas without being subject to censorship or intervention from the government. The preservation of free speech has been an essential component of democracy throughout the entirety of the history of the United States of America. This has made it possible for open conversation, dissent, and the interchange of ideas.

However, extreme leftist elitist organizations have been advocating for limits on free speech in some settings for a growing number of years. Hate speech, insulting rhetoric, and sentiments that promote structural injustices are all things that they think should be restricted. This has resulted in discussions and disagreements over questions such as the following:

1. Campus Speech Codes

On college campuses, the debate over speech regulations and "safe spaces" has become a contentious subject between students and faculty. According to Volokh (2012), many believe that these regulations are required to safeguard disadvantaged groups from potential harm, while others consider them to be violations of academic freedom and freedom of expression.

2. Online Censorship

Concerns have been expressed over the role that social media platforms and technology corporations play in the regulation of content as a result of their impact. Concerns have been raised over the possibility of the suppression of voices that disagree with the status quo as a result of calls for the elimination of hate speech and disinformation (Volokh, 2012).

3. Cancel Culture

An issue that has proven problematic is the phenomenon known as "cancel culture," which entails the public shaming and boycotting of persons or groups who are believed to possess unacceptable ideas. An argument that has been made against it is that it inhibits open debate and promotes self-censorship (Volokh, 2012).

4. The Marketplace of Ideas

The concept of a "marketplace of ideas," in which different points of view are permitted to freely compete with one another, has been called into question by those who believe that some points of view need to be prohibited to safeguard underrepresented groups (Volokh, 2012).

The Right to Bear Arms

Following the United States Constitution (n.d.), the Second Amendment safeguards the right of individuals to possess and carry firearms. Self-defense, personal liberty, and protection against tyranny are frequently connected with this right, which has significant historical origins in the United States and is frequently related to freedom of expression. There has been a great deal of discussion and interpretation of the law about this matter.

In the pretext of minimizing gun violence and protecting public safety, radical leftist elitist groups have advocated for increasingly stringent measures to regulate the availability of firearms. A battle of views has resulted as a result of this, with supporters of gun rights contending that any limits placed on the Second Amendment violate their liberties. Controversial issues include the following:

1. Assault Weapons Bans

There have been disputes over the extent of the rights afforded by the Second Amendment as a result of debates around the prohibition of assault weapons, high-capacity magazines, and certain attachments for firearms (Kates & Mauser, 2007).

2. Background Checks

Discussions on the appropriate balance between avoiding gun violence and respecting the rights of law-abiding gun owners have been generated by efforts to increase background checks for the purchase of firearms (Kates & Mauser, 2007).

3. Red Flag Laws

Concerns over due process and the possibility of misuse have been raised as a result of the introduction of red flag legislation, which permit the temporary seizure of guns from persons who are believed to represent a threat (Kates & Mauser, 2007).

Privacy and Surveillance

Although it is not specifically specified in the Constitution, the right to privacy has been acknowledged and safeguarded by the Supreme Court (Solove, 2006). The protection of personal information, the freedom from unlawful searches and seizures, and the right to be secure in one's own home are all included in this concept.

Concerns over privacy have been more prevalent in recent years as a result of the progression of technology. There are legitimate concerns that have been made by radical leftist elitist organizations over the collection of data and monitoring by the government. On the other hand, the solutions that they suggest come into conflict with the ideals of individual liberty rather frequently. One example of this is the rising regulation of technology businesses. The following are main areas of concern:

1. Data Privacy

There have been concerns voiced on the necessity of regulation to safeguard individuals from the possibility of abuse as a result of the gathering and sharing of personal data by technology businesses (Solove, 2006).

2. Government Surveillance

Discussions regarding government surveillance programs, such as the gathering of metadata and the monitoring of online conversations, have brought to light the conflict that exists between the protection of civil rights and the protection of national security (Solove, 2006).

3. Encryption

There have been discussions on whether or not law enforcement should have access to encrypted data to conduct criminal investigations (Solove, 2006). These discussions have been triggered by the usage of strong encryption to secure personal communications.

Due Process and Criminal Justice

It is the responsibility of the government to ensure that citizens are afforded judicial processes that are both fair and unbiased. Due process is guaranteed under the Fifth and Fourteenth Amendments. According to the United States Constitution (n.d.), it encompasses the right to a fair trial, the right to legal representation, and the right to be protected from incriminating oneself.

There are concerns of systematic unfairness within the criminal justice system, notably about racial inequality, and radical leftist elitist groups have brought attention to these issues. On the other hand, their proposed solutions, which include defunding the police or altering bail systems, have generated worries about the possible impact on due process and public safety. These concerns are genuine, but their proposed solutions have created difficulties. The following are the main sources of tension:

1. Police Reform

The efforts that have been made to improve policing methods and address concerns about police brutality have led to conversations regarding the balance that should be struck between protecting the public and protecting individual rights (Pfaff, 2017).

2. Bail Reform

Concerns regarding public safety and the rights of crime victims have been at the center of discussions on the introduction of bail reform and the release of individuals who are currently awaiting trial (Pfaff, 2017).

3. Sentencing and Rehabilitation

Pfaff (2017) notes that talks on the rights of victims and the possible hazards of early release have been triggered by calls for sentencing reform and an emphasis on rehabilitation rather than punishment.

The Impact on Society

A wide variety of implications and debates have arisen as a result of the assault on individual rights that has been carried out by extreme leftist elitist groups:

1. Balancing Rights and Responsibilities

During conversations regarding issues such as free speech, gun control, privacy, and reforming the criminal justice system, the tension that exists between individual rights and society's responsibilities has emerged as a prevalent topic of debate.

2. Legal Challenges

Legal challenges and historic cases brought before the Supreme Court have been brought about as a result of proposed limits on individual rights (Liptak, 2020). certain cases aim to establish the bounds of certain types of rights.

3. Ideological Polarization

It is difficult to identify common ground and reach an agreement on important problems as a result of ideological polarization, which has been contributed to by debates regarding individual rights.

4. Public Opinion

Discussions regarding the changing role of government and the rights of individuals in a society that is changing have been triggered by the erosion of individual rights.

Conclusion of Part 1

As we get to the end of the first part of "The Erosion of Freedom," it is abundantly clear that the attack on individual rights by radical leftist elitist organizations has sparked a variety of complicated and heated arguments regarding the appropriate balance between safeguarding fundamental liberties and solving social difficulties. In the next sections of this chapter, we will look into more aspects of their influence on the American ideal. We will investigate the deterioration of economic freedom, the promotion of collectivism, and the larger ramifications for the future of the United States of America.

References:

U.S. Constitution. (n.d.). The Constitution of the United States. National Archives. Retrieved from https://www.archives.gov/founding-docs/constitution

Volokh, E. (2012). Freedom of Speech and Intellectual Property: Some Thoughts After Golan and Knox. Emory Law Journal, 61(5), 1087-1110.

Kates, D. B., & Mauser, G. (2007). Would Banning Firearms Reduce Murder and Suicide? A Review of International Evidence. Harvard Journal of Law & Public Policy, 30(2), 649-694.

Solove, D. J. (2006). A Taxonomy of Privacy. University of Pennsylvania Law Review, 154(3), 477-564.

Pfaff, J. F. (2017). Locked In: The True Causes of Mass Incarceration and How to Achieve Real Reform. Basic Books.

Liptak, A. (2020). Supreme Court Backs Payments to Student-Athletes in N.C.A.A. Case. The New York Times. Retrieved from https://www.nytimes.com/2021/06/30/us/supreme-court-ncaa-athletes.html

Part 2: The Assault on Capitalism

As part of our continuous investigation of the influence that radical leftist elitist groups have had on the American dream and the larger social landscape of the United States, we are now going to focus on an essential component of their goal, which is the assault on capitalism. The economic system that has been the foundation of American wealth for a very long time, capitalism has been the system that has fostered innovation, entrepreneurialism, and economic progress. On the other hand, extreme leftist elitist organizations have been increasingly challenging the core foundations of capitalism and arguing for a shift toward alternative economic models. This chapter takes a look at the various ways in which capitalism is being challenged, the reasons that are driving these challenges, and the possible repercussions that these difficulties might have for the American ideal.

The Foundation of American Prosperity: Capitalism

Capitalism, which is distinguished by the private ownership of the means of production, market competition, and businesses that are driven by profit, has been an essential component in the process of sculpting the economic landscape of the United States (Smith, 1776). Promoting an atmosphere in which individuals and businesses can innovate, generate wealth, and follow their economic dreams, it has been a driving force behind the unprecedented economic growth that the nation has seen.

1. Entrepreneurship and Innovation

The fostering of entrepreneurialism and invention is one of the defining characteristics of the capitalist economic system. The liberty to establish new firms, create innovative goods, and compete in the market has resulted in the development of ground-breaking innovations in a variety of fields, including medicine, technology, and manufacturing. From the beginning of the American dream, entrepreneurs and inventors have been at the vanguard, generating possibilities not just for themselves but also for future generations.

2. Economic Mobility

Individuals have been able to better their financial situations via the application of hard effort and invention thanks to capitalism, which has traditionally offered a road for economic mobility (Smith, 1776). Throughout the history of the American dream, the concept of "rags to riches" has been a key motif. This concept reflects the possibility that people from a variety of backgrounds might attain success.

3. Market Efficiency

According to Smith (1776), market competition in capitalism promotes resource allocation that is based on customer demand, as well as efficiency and cost-effectiveness in the distribution of resources. This efficiency has resulted in an increase in the population's standard of living as well as an expansion in the range of products and services that are offered to customers.

4. Wealth Creation

Because capitalism is driven by profit, it has made it easier for people to accumulate money, which has been to the advantage of business owners as well as investors (Smith, 1776). Philanthropy, the creation of jobs, and investments in research and development have all been made possible as a result of this wealth creation.

Some extreme leftist elitist organizations, on the other hand, argue that capitalism is responsible for the perpetuation of structural inequities, the concentration of wealth in the hands of a select few, and the worsening of social gaps. They contend that the quest of profit in capitalism may result in immoral corporate practices, environmental destruction, and exploitation of people and animals. As a consequence of this, they have begun an assault on capitalism, looking for alternative economic models that place a higher priority on social justice and fairness.

The Assault on Capitalism

The attack on capitalism that is being carried out by extreme leftist elitist organizations can take many different forms. Each of these forms is designed to challenge the fundamental foundations of the economic system and to advocate for alternative models.

1. Wealth Redistribution

Redistribution of wealth is one of the primary goals that these organizations strive to achieve. According to Piketty (2014), they advocate for more taxes on the affluent, increased government engagement in the economy, and social welfare programs that are aimed at minimizing income and wealth inequality.

2. Socialism and Marxism

Marx and Engels (1848) state that certain radical leftist elitist groups openly support socialism and Marxism as alternatives to capitalism at the same time. In addition to advocating for the nationalization of important businesses, they advocate for the elimination of private property and the construction of an economic system that is more egalitarian.

3. Advocacy for Workers' Rights

To achieve their goals, these organizations frequently engage in activities that aim to enhance labor unions and workers' rights. According to Card (1992), they advocate for increased minimum salaries, rights to collective bargaining, and rules in the workplace that are designed to improve working conditions for employed individuals.

4. Environmental and Social Responsibility

Those who advocate for responsible capitalism encourage firms to take responsibility for their impact on the environment and society. According to Porter and Kramer (2011), they advise businesses to become involved in charitable endeavors and social projects, as well as to take into consideration the influence that their operations have on the environment.

5. Critique of Corporate Power

There is a common practice among radical leftist elitist organizations to criticize the strength and influence of huge businesses in dictating the policies of the government and the outcomes of the economy. Specifically, they advocate for higher responsibility and more stringent controls to be placed on businesses (Stigler, 1971).

The Motivations Behind the Assault

It is vital to have a solid understanding of the driving factors behind these issues to have a complete comprehension of the motives underlying the assault on capitalism. The following is a condensed version of the reasons that extreme leftist elitist groups take their actions:

1. Social Justice

The quest for social justice is one of the primary drivers of motivation. These groups contend that capitalism is responsible for the perpetuation of inequalities and inequities, and they strive to repair these perceived injustices by campaigning for fair economic policies and the transfer of wealth (Rawls, 1971).

2. Environmental Concerns

Certain groups are motivated to advocate for a more ecologically responsible economic system (Piketty, 2014). These groups are motivated by concerns regarding the sustainability of the environment and the influence that unregulated capitalism has on the globe.

3. Worker Empowerment

To empower workers and solve the issue of economic disparity, organizations that advocate for workers' rights and stronger labor unions are taking action (Card, 1992).

4. Opposition to Corporate Influence

Calls for stronger regulation and accountability are being driven by criticisms of the power and influence of companies (Stigler, 1971). These criticisms are intended to prevent businesses from influencing the results of economic and political processes.

The Potential Consequences

The assault on capitalism has the potential to have repercussions for the American ideal as well as the economic landscape of the United States as a whole:

1. Economic Efficiency

According to Smith (1776), these challenges to capitalism have the potential to affect economic efficiency by establishing rules and policies that impede market competition and innovation.

2. Wealth Creation

The goal of wealth redistribution might hinder entrepreneurial endeavors and the development of wealth, which could potentially slow down economic progress (Smith, 1776).

3. Job Creation

According to Stigler (1971), more regulation and corporate monitoring may have an impact on the creation of new jobs as well as the general health of the labor market.

4. Innovation

According to Smith (1776), a move away from capitalism might potentially weaken the incentives for scientific discovery and technological progress.

5. Economic Freedom

It is possible that the emphasis that capitalism places on economic freedom would decrease, which might have repercussions for the economic autonomy of individuals and the pursuit of the American ideal (Smith, 1776).

Conclusion of Part 2

In concluding Part 2 of "The Erosion of Freedom," we have examined the assault on capitalism by radical leftist elitist groups, exploring the motivations behind their challenges and the potential consequences for the American dream and the broader economic landscape. The next sections of this chapter will delve into the promotion of collectivism, the erosion of freedom, and the broader implications for the future of America.

References:

Smith, A. (1776). An Inquiry into the Nature and Causes of the Wealth of Nations. London: W. Strahan and T. Cadell.

Marx, K., & Engels, F. (1848). The Communist Manifesto. London: League of the Just.

Piketty, T. (2014). Capital in the Twenty-First Century. Harvard University Press.

Card, D. (1992). Do Minimum Wages Reduce Employment? A Case Study of California, 1987-1989. Industrial and Labor Relations Review, 46(1), 38-54.

Porter, M. E., & Kramer, M. R. (2011). Creating Shared Value. Harvard Business Review, 89(1-2), 62-77.

Rawls, J. (1971). A Theory of Justice. Harvard University Press.

Stigler, G. J. (1971). The Theory of Economic Regulation. The Bell Journal of Economics and Management Science, 2(1), 3-21.

Part 3: The Promotion of Collectivism

As part of our continuous investigation into the influence that radical leftist elitist groups have had on the American dream and the larger social landscape of the United States, we are now going to focus on an essential component of their plan, which is the promotion of collectivism. The term "collectivism" refers to a socio-economic and political philosophy that emphasizes the redistribution of wealth, the common ownership of resources, and shared responsibility for the well-being of society. In spite of the fact that collectivism has its supporters and has been implemented in a variety of ways in a number of nations, extreme leftist elitist organizations have been increasingly advocating for collectivist ideals in the United States. This chapter investigates the many means by which collectivism is being pushed forward, the reasons that are driving this movement, and the potential repercussions that this movement may have for the American ideal.

The American Dream and Individualism

Throughout history, the concept of individualism has been closely linked to the American ideal. Individualism refers to the notion that people should be able to follow their own goals, desires, and pleasure. According to Bellah et al. (1985), the ideology of individualism has been a distinguishing characteristic of American society. It has contributed to the development of a culture that values self-reliance, entrepreneurialism, and personal accomplishment.

1. Economic Individualism

As an example of economic individualism, the conviction that people have the freedom to possess private property, establish their enterprises, and enjoy the results of their labor is a good example. Since its inception, capitalism has been the economic system that has been most closely associated with this individualistic attitude (Smith, 1776). Capitalism places heavy emphasis on private enterprise and competition.

2. Personal Liberty

One other fundamental component of the American ideal is the concept of personal liberty. The United States Constitution (n.d.), comprises the freedom to make decisions on one's life, to seek education, to select a career, and to practice religion or hold views without interference from unreasonable authorities.

3. Social Mobility

One of the most important aspects of the American dream is social mobility, which may be defined as the capacity to enhance one's economic and social status via the application of effort and talent. According to Smith (1776), one of the most potent motivators is the strong conviction that individuals are capable of overcoming challenges and achieving success.

4. Limited Government

The concept of the "American dream" has frequently been linked to the idea that the government should intervene in the lives of individuals and corporations to a limited extent. According to Locke (1689), the concept that individuals should have the ability to make choices and mold their destinies with little intervention is the foundation of the principle of limited government.

The Promotion of Collectivism

Certain radical leftist elitist groups have posed a threat to the individualistic philosophy that underpins the American ideal, and they have advocated for collectivist ideas and policies. They promote collectivism in a variety of ways, including the following:

1. Wealth Redistribution

One of the fundamental principles that underpin collectivism is the redistribution of wealth. These organizations put up the argument that money and resources ought to be allocated among the people more equitably. This typically results in requests for increased taxes to be levied on the rich as well as the establishment of social assistance programs (Piketty, 2014).

2. Social Safety Nets

The significance of strong social safety nets to safeguard disadvantaged members of society is emphasized by those who advocate for collectivism. They advocate for the extension of services such as healthcare, education, and housing to guarantee that all individuals have access to the fundamental requirements (Esping-Andersen, 1990).

3. Economic Planning

Certain extreme leftist elitist groups support economic planning and the centralization of decision-making in the economic sphere. In their argument, they contend that a more equitable distribution of income and resources may be achieved through the community ownership of important businesses and resources (Hayek, 1945).

4. Worker Ownership

Traditional capitalist businesses are being challenged by the promotion of worker ownership and cooperatives as viable alternatives. The models in question emphasize employee participation in decision-making and shared ownership (Birchall, 2011).

5. Government Regulation

Collectivist advocacy encompasses some different forms, one of which is called for stronger government control of the economy. These organizations contend that the involvement of the government is essential to correct market failures, protect consumers, and guarantee justice (Keynes, 1936).

The Motivations Behind the Promotion

Gaining an understanding of the extreme leftist elitist groups' objective requires first and foremost an understanding of the rationale underlying the promotion of collectivism by these groups. To summarize the motivations, the following is what they are:

1. Social Justice

The quest for social justice and the elimination of gaps in income and wealth are two of the most important motives. According to Rawls (1971), these organizations contend that collectivist policies are necessary to rectify systemic injustices and to advance the cause of fairness.

2. Economic Equality

According to Esping-Andersen (1990), proponents of collectivism place a high priority on economic equality as a method of guaranteeing that all members of society have access to opportunities and resources that are necessary for their survival.

3. Public Welfare

Motivation for the promotion of collectivism comes from a dedication to ensuring the health and happiness of all citizens. According to Rawls (1971), these organizations contend that to meet the requirements of the entire population, it is essential to engage in collective action and to exercise shared responsibility.

4. Environmental Sustainability

[Rawls, 1971] asserts that the need for collectivist measures to handle environmental difficulties is driven by concerns for the long-term viability of the environment and the environmentally appropriate use of resources.

The Potential Consequences

The promotion of collectivism may have repercussions for the American dream as well as for the larger social and economic environment of the United States, including the following:

1. Economic Efficiency

Hayek (1945) suggests that it is possible for more government intervention and economic planning to affect economic efficiency and creativity.

2. Individual Autonomy

According to Locke (1689), collectivist policies have the potential to have an impact on individual autonomy and the capacity of individuals to make decisions regarding their lives.

3. Wealth Redistribution

There is a possibility that the introduction of laws that redistribute money might inhibit entrepreneurial endeavors and the production of wealth (Smith, 1776).

4. Government Dependency

Esping-Andersen (1990) suggests that an increase in the population's reliance on the government might result from the expansion of social safety nets and services being supplied by the government.

5. Ideological Division

The promotion of collectivism has the potential to widen ideological differences within American society, as arguments about the role of government and individual responsibility grow (Bellah et al., 1985). This is because collectivism is becoming increasingly popular.

Conclusion of Part 3

As we come to the end of Part 3 of "The Erosion of Freedom," it is abundantly clear that the advocacy of collectivism by radical leftist elitist groups is a substantial divergence from the individualistic philosophy that has been linked with the American ideal for a considerable amount of time. As we move further in this chapter, we will look more into the deterioration of freedom and the wider ramifications that this has for the future of the United States of America.

References:

Bellah, R. N., Madsen, R., Sullivan, W. M., Swidler, A., & Tipton, S. M. (1985). Habits of the Heart: Individualism and Commitment in American Life. University of California Press.

Esping-Andersen, G. (1990). The Three Worlds of Welfare Capitalism. Princeton University Press.

Hayek, F. A. (1945). The Use of Knowledge in Society. The American Economic Review, 35(4), 519-530.

Keynes, J. M. (1936). The General Theory of Employment, Interest and Money. Macmillan.

Locke, J. (1689). Two Treatises of Government. A. Millar, J. and R. Tonson, H. Woodfall, J. Rivington, et al.

Marx, K., & Engels, F. (1848). The Communist Manifesto. London: League of the Just.

Piketty, T. (2014). Capital in the Twenty-First Century. Harvard University Press.

Rawls, J. (1971). A Theory of Justice. Harvard University Press.

Smith, A. (1776). An Inquiry into the Nature and Causes of the Wealth of Nations. London: W. Strahan and T. Cadell.

Part 4: The Erosion of Freedom

As we continue our investigation into the influence that radical leftist elitist groups have had on the American dream and the larger landscape of American society, we are now going to focus on an essential component of their objective, which is the deterioration of freedom. Freedom, which encompasses individual rights, minimal government intrusion, and the opportunity to achieve one's dreams, has been a basic cornerstone of American culture for a very long time. On the other hand, extreme leftist elitist organizations have been progressively challenging these ideals and demanding further government control and regulation. In this chapter, we investigate the various ways in which freedom is being eroded, the reasons that are driving this erosion, and the potential repercussions that this loss may have for the American ideal.

The American Dream and Freedom

Since the beginning of the United States of America, the idea of freedom has been an essential component of the American dream. It is the embodiment of the concept that people have the freedom to make decisions about their lives, to enjoy personal rights, and to pursue their own sense of pleasure regardless of the circumstances.

1. Individual Liberties

According to the United States Constitution (n.d.), individual freedoms encompass the rights that are incorporated in the Constitution of the United States of America. These rights include freedom of speech, freedom of religion, freedom of assembly, and the right to carry weapons. The American democracy has always been built on the foundation of these rights.

2. Limited Government

The concept of limited government is fundamental to the spirit of the American ideal. It emphasizes the fact that the function of the government ought to be limited, with minimum involvement in the lives of individuals and enterprises. According to Locke (1689), this notion is founded on the idea that people ought to be able to independently choose their destiny and make decisions about their lives.

3. Pursuit of Aspirations

The concept of the "American dream" inspires people to work toward achieving their goals and reaching their potential. According to Smith (1776), it is a celebration of the concept that everyone can achieve success and enhance their quality of life if they are willing to put in a lot of effort, be determined, and be creative.

4. Economic Freedom

In the context of economic freedom, which is strongly associated with capitalism, people are granted the ability to own property, establish enterprises, and engage in commercial activities with minimum intervention from the government (Smith, 1776). The freedom in question has been an essential component of economic success.

The Erosion of Freedom

The ideals of freedom have been the target of an assault from radical leftist elitist groups, which have advocated for policies and acts that undermine these fundamental values. Liberties are being eroded in a variety of ways, including:

1. Expansion of Government Power

Increasing the authority of the government and interfering in many different parts of people's lives is one of the key factors that is contributing to the erosion of freedom. According to Keynes (1936), these organizations argue for increased government control in a variety of disciplines, including healthcare, education, and the economy.

2. Suppression of Free Speech

According to Mill (1859), certain extreme leftist elitist parties have been attacked for their suppression of free speech and promotion of cancel culture, both of which impede open conversation and perspectives that are different from one another.

3. Gun Control

A topic that has been the subject of debate is the implementation of more stringent gun control laws. others who support these restrictions claim that they are essential for the protection of the general public, while others who oppose them consider them to be a danger to the Second Amendment (Lott, 2000).

4. Economic Regulation

There is a widespread tendency among these organizations to advocate for higher economic regulation and taxation applied to enterprises and individuals with high incomes. Specifically, they claim that such policies are necessary to address the issue of economic inequality (Piketty, 2014).

5. Identity Politics

Many organizations have utilized identity politics, which emphasizes the identities and grievances of groups, to achieve their objectives. Some people believe that it can be detrimental to individual liberties since it places a higher value on communal identities than it does on individual rights (Haidt, 2018).

The Motivations Behind the Erosion

In order to comprehend the purpose of extreme leftist elitist groups, it is vital to have an understanding of the causes behind the erosion of freedom brought about by these groups. To summarize the motivations, the following is what they are:

1. Social Justice

The relentless pursuit of social justice and equality is a primary driving force behind the gradual loss of individual liberty. According to Rawls (1971), these organizations contend that to solve the issue of structural inequalities, it is essential to take measures such as redistribution of wealth and increased government engagement.

2. Public Welfare

The well-being of the general people is given the utmost importance by followers of the erosion of freedom. They say that it is vital for the government to intervene in sectors such as education and healthcare to guarantee that all citizens have access to the basic services that they require (Rawls, 1971).

3. Gun Violence Prevention

The worries regarding gun violence and the safety of the general population are the driving force behind the efforts to establish stronger gun control laws. Those who support the idea claim that such steps are necessary to lessen the number of people who own weapons (Lott, 2000).

4. Protection from Hate Speech

In many cases, the suppression of free speech is justified as a means of protecting individuals from damaging rhetoric and hate speech. Those who advocate for this approach are of the opinion that it is essential in order to avoid causing harm and prejudice; Mill (1859).

5. Economic Equality

The aim to decrease economic gaps and to promote economic equality is the driving force behind calls for higher economic regulation and taxes (Piketty, 2014).

The Potential Consequences

There is the possibility that the erosion of freedom will have repercussions for the American ideal as well as for the larger social and political landscape:

1. Individual Liberties

According to the United States Constitution (n.d.), the erosion of freedom can lead to restrictions on individual freedoms, which may infringe upon rights that are guaranteed by the Constitution of the United States of America.

2. Limited Government

The idea of limited government may be challenged by expanding the power and interference of the government, which would result in a shift in the equilibrium between individual and state authority (Locke, 1689).

3. Economic Prosperity

According to Smith (1776), rising levels of economic regulation and taxes can affect economic success and entrepreneurial activity.

4. Free Speech

According to Mill (1859), the elimination of the right to free speech has the potential to impede open conversation and restrict the variety of ideas and points of view.

5. Political Polarization

At the same time as discussions about the role of government get more heated, the degradation of freedom can make political polarization even more pronounced (Haidt, 2018).

Conclusion of Part 4

As we get to the end of Part 4 of "The Erosion of Freedom," it is abundantly clear that the erosion of freedom by radical leftist elitist organizations constitutes a considerable divergence from the ideas that have been linked with the American dream for a very long time. The subsequent sections of this chapter will investigate the more far-reaching ramifications for the future of the United States of America, taking into consideration the deterioration of traditional values and the general course of the nation.

References:

Haidt, J. (2018). The Coddling of the American Mind: How Good Intentions and Bad Ideas Are Setting Up a Generation for Failure. Penguin Press.

Keynes, J. M. (1936). The General Theory of Employment, Interest and Money. Macmillan.

Locke, J. (1689). Two Treatises of Government. A. Millar, J. and R. Tonson, H. Woodfall, J. Rivington, et al.

Lott, J. R. (2000). More Guns, Less Crime: Understanding Crime and Gun Control Laws. University of Chicago Press.

Mill, J. S. (1859). On Liberty. John W. Parker and Son.

Piketty, T. (2014). Capital in the Twenty-First Century. Harvard University Press.

Rawls, J. (1971). A Theory of Justice. Harvard University Press.

Smith, A. (1776). An Inquiry into the Nature and Causes of the Wealth of Nations. London: W. Strahan and T. Cadell.

U.S. Constitution. (n.d.). The Constitution of the United States. National Archives and Records Administration.

Part 5: The Impact on Society

As we continue our exploration of the impact of radical leftist elitist groups on the American dream and the broader social fabric of the United States, it is essential to delve into the consequences of their actions and policies on society. The deterioration of individual liberty and the encouragement of collectivism, both of which were covered in earlier parts, have far-reaching ramifications for a variety of areas of life in the United States. In this section, we will investigate the enormous effects that these developments have had on society, ranging from cultural upheavals to political polarization and the overall well-being of the nation as a whole.

Cultural Shifts

The policies and ideals that are advocated by extreme leftist elitist groups have been a significant contributor to the cultural alterations that have taken place in American culture. These changes are defined by transformations in attitudes, values, and conventions that impact the way people interact with one another and engage with their communities. These shifts were brought about by a combination of factors.

1. Identity Politics

An increased emphasis on group identities, such as those about race, gender, and sexuality, has resulted from the growth of identity politics, which has been championed by some of these distinct groups. While this strategy has been attacked for generating a "us versus them" mentality and stressing divisions, it has also been condemned for calling for greater social justice and inclusivity (Haidt, 2018).

2. Cancel Culture

Cancel culture, which is frequently connected with the suppression of alternative viewpoints and the holding of individuals or institutions accountable for perceived wrongs, has emerged as a key aspect of both online and offline conversation. On the other hand, detractors see it as a danger to free speech and open discourse (Haidt, 2018). Proponents of the measure claim that it acts as a tool for accountability.

3. Shifting Moral Values

In areas such as social justice, ecology, and the prioritization of collective well-being over individual rights, there has been a discernible shift in the moral ideals that are held. According to Rawls (1971), these adjustments are a reflection of the shifting norms and attitudes of society.

Political Polarization

The influence of extreme leftist elitist groups extends into the realm of politics, which contributes to the heightened political polarization and division that exists throughout American society.

1. Ideological Polarization

The widening gap between liberal and conservative points of view is a defining characteristic of ideological polarization. The propagation of collectivist and communist ideology has, according to Haidt (2018), contributed to the escalation of tensions with individuals who advocate for limited government and individual liberty.

2. Partisan Gridlock

Political stalemate has emerged as a consequence of the division that has occurred in American politics. This has made it increasingly challenging for legislators to find areas of agreement and to pass important legislation. According to Haidt (2018), this impasse makes it difficult to make progress on the most important topics, such as healthcare and immigration reform.

3. Fragmented Media Landscape

As a result of news outlets catering to specific ideological audiences, the landscape of the media has become more fragmented and polarized. Because of this fragmentation, preexisting ideas may be strengthened, and exposure to a variety of perspectives may be restricted (Haidt, 2018).

Social Well-Being

The policies that are supported by radical leftist elitist groups have repercussions for the overall well-being of American society. These policies have an impact on a variety of aspects, including the stability of the economy, the health of the public, and the educational opportunities available.

1. Economic Stability

Although policies that try to redistribute wealth and regulate the economy are intended to alleviate inequality, they also have the potential to affect economic stability and the entrepreneurial spirit that has traditionally been the driving force behind the prosperity of the United States (Smith, 1776).

2. Healthcare Access

It is possible that outcomes related to public health could be improved and inequities could be reduced if efforts were made to broaden access to healthcare. (Rawls, 1971) However, the influence of such policies on the quality of healthcare, the affordability of healthcare, and the choice of healthcare continues to be a topic of controversy.

3. Education

The argument that higher government intervention in education can lead to greater equity in educational opportunities is put up by proponents of this intervention. On the other hand, there are ongoing discussions over the efficacy of such interventions and the influence they have on the outcomes of educational endeavors (Rawls, 1971).

4. Environmental Sustainability

The environmental policies that are supported by some of these organizations are designed to address the urgent environmental problems that exist today. Furthermore, the trade-offs that exist between the protection of the environment and the expansion of the economy are a topic that is always being discussed (Rawls, 1971).

Conclusion of Part 5

In concluding Part 5 of "The Erosion of Freedom," it is evident that the impact of radical leftist elitist groups on American society is multifaceted and extends across various domains, from culture and politics to social well-being. The next section of this chapter will provide a comprehensive overview of the consequences of these changes and their potential long-term effects on the American dream and the future of the nation.

References:

Haidt, J. (2018). The Coddling of the American Mind: How Good Intentions and Bad Ideas Are Setting Up a Generation for Failure. Penguin Press.

Rawls, J. (1971). A Theory of Justice. Harvard University Press.

Smith, A. (1776). An Inquiry into the Nature and Causes of the Wealth of Nations. London: W. Strahan and T. Cadell.

Part 6: Conclusion

We have gone into the degradation of freedom, the promotion of collectivism, and the far-reaching ramifications of these phenomena as part of an in-depth investigation of the impact that extreme leftist elitist groups have had on the American dream and the larger societal landscape of the United States. As we get to the end of this chapter, it is crucial to summarize the most important findings, evaluate the consequences of these changes, and contemplate the possibilities for the future of the United States of America in light of these developments.

Recap of Key Insights

During this chapter, we have uncovered several significant revelations concerning the activities and policies of radical leftist elitist groups, including the following:

Erosion of Freedom

In the United States, the expansion of government authority, the restriction of free expression, efforts to enforce stronger gun control measures, more economic regulation, and the emergence of identity politics have all contributed to the erosion of freedom, which is a basic pillar of the American ideal. These changes pose a threat to the ideas of individual liberty, limited government, and economic independence that have traditionally been the defining characteristics of American society at large.

Promotion of Collectivism

Through the promotion of collectivism, which is championed by these groups, income redistribution, the growth of social safety nets, economic planning, worker ownership, and increasing government regulation are all included. The proponents of these measures say that they are necessary to achieve social justice, economic equality, public welfare, and environmental sustainability.

Motivations

The quest for social justice, economic equality, public welfare, protection from hate speech, and environmental sustainability are the driving forces behind the erosion of freedom and the promotion of collectivism. These are the objectives that provide the foundation for these developments. Even though these ideas have great intentions, they have been the subject of a significant amount of dispute and controversy.

Consequences

The repercussions of these shifts are significant and complicated in many different ways. Changes in culture have resulted in the emergence of identity politics and cancel culture, which have had an impact on how individuals interact with society and communicate their thoughts. As a result of the intensification of political polarization, ideological divides and partisan deadlock have emerged respectively. The alterations that occur in economic stability, access to healthcare, educational possibilities, and environmental sustainability all affect the social well-being of individuals.

Implications and Controversies

In the continuous debate and controversy that surrounds the topic, the ramifications of the acts and policies of extreme leftist elitist groups are a matter of discussion. Others are concerned about the erosion of individual liberties, economic efficiency, and the potential repercussions of expanded government interference. While some people argue that these reforms are required to address systemic disparities and social injustices, others express their concerns about the potential ramifications of expanded government intervention.

Balancing Freedom and Equality

One of the most significant obstacles that must be overcome to successfully navigate this terrain is to find a middle ground between protecting individual liberties and fostering greater equality. Several policy disputes in the United States of America today are centered on the conflict that exists between these two values.

Protecting Free Speech

Debates over the limitations of free expression and the necessity of protecting dissenting ideas while addressing hate speech and damaging language have been sparked as a result of the suppression of free speech, which is frequently associated with cancel culture and online censorship.

Economic Prosperity vs. Regulation

It is still a contested question whether or not there should be a trade-off between higher government regulation and economic development.

Opponents of regulation express concerns about the possible stifling effect it could have on entrepreneurialism and innovation, while proponents of regulation believe that it is necessary for reducing economic inequality.

Environmental Responsibility

When it comes to resolving urgent ecological concerns, it is necessary to own environmental regulations that are geared toward sustainability and responsible resource management. Nevertheless, the way forward requires making difficult choices regarding the appropriate balance between the protection of the environment and the expansion of the economy.

The Future of America

Important problems regarding the future of the United States of America are raised as a result of the influence that extreme leftist elitist groups have had on the American dream and society as a whole. As the nation struggles to adapt to these shifts, it must ponder how it may maintain its fundamental principles while simultaneously tackling the urgent problems that are confronting society.

Bridging Divides

The efforts that are made to bridge gaps and develop constructive conversation are vital to successfully manage the obstacles that are posed by political polarization and ideological conflicts. When it comes to important subjects, finding common ground and encouraging civil discourse can help reduce division.

Protecting Liberties

The concepts of limited government, the protection of individual liberties, and the right to freedom of speech continue to be vital to the American experience. Maintaining a healthy equilibrium between these ideals and the goal of social justice and equality will continue to be a primary focus in the governing process in the United States.

Fostering Innovation

It is a difficult effort to overcome the challenge of reducing economic inequality while also fostering innovation and economic growth. The regulatory environment and the impact it has on entrepreneurial endeavors are two factors that policymakers need to carefully evaluate.

Environmental Sustainability

A holistic approach that includes responsible resource management, technological innovation, and international cooperation is required to address environmental concerns while also supporting economic growth.

Conclusion

In concluding this chapter on "The Erosion of Freedom," it is evident that the actions and policies of radical leftist elitist groups have had a profound impact on American society. These changes raise complex questions about the balance between individual liberties and collective well-being, the boundaries of free speech, and the trade-offs between economic prosperity and regulation.

As America moves forward, it must grapple with these challenges and seek solutions that preserve its core values while addressing pressing issues. Finding common ground, protecting individual liberties, fostering innovation, and promoting environmental responsibility will be crucial steps in shaping the future of the nation.

References:

Haidt, J. (2018). The Coddling of the American Mind: How Good Intentions and Bad Ideas Are Setting Up a Generation for Failure. Penguin Press.

Locke, J. (1689). Two Treatises of Government. A. Millar, J. and R. Tonson, H. Woodfall, J. Rivington, et al.

Rawls, J. (1971). A Theory of Justice. Harvard University Press.

Smith, A. (1776). An Inquiry into the Nature and Causes of the Wealth of Nations. London: W. Strahan and T. Cadell.

Chapter 4: The Rise of Resistance

"THE AWAKENING OF THE SILENT MAJORITY"

Chapter 4 explores the growing resistance against radical leftist elitist groups and their Socialist-State. As Americans from all walks of life come to realize the danger posed by these groups, they unite in a collective effort to safeguard the nation's future. This chapter delves into the rise of conservative and patriotic movements, highlighting their strategies and the profound impact they have on the political landscape.

Chapter Outline:

1. The Conservative Awakening

2. The Birth of Patriotic Movements

3. The Rise of Independent Media

4. The Social Media Counteroffensive

5. The Impact on Society

6. Conclusion

Part 1: The Conservative Awakening

This chapter marks the beginning of a trip that will take us on an exploration of the astonishing rebirth of conservative and patriotic movements as a reaction to the growing influence of extreme leftist elitist groups and their vision of a socialist state. The political landscape is being shaped by these movements, which are playing a vital role in challenging the status quo as they gather momentum within the political environment. In this section, we will investigate the beginnings, techniques, and tremendous effects that this conservative awakening has had on the society of the United States.

The Call to Action

A response to the perceived challenges posed by the rise of extreme leftist elitist groups campaigning for a socialist state, the conservative awakening in the United States of America takes place as a result of this. In recent years, these organizations have become more vociferous in their demands for increased government control, the transfer of wealth, and the reduction of individual liberties. As a result of these issues, a large number of people from a variety of different backgrounds in the United States have been forced to take action to save the values that they hold dear.

A Diverse Coalition

One of the most astonishing aspects of the conservative awakening is the fact that people from a wide variety of backgrounds and voices have come together to build a unified front. There is a wide variety of ideological backgrounds among conservatives, ranging from libertarians who emphasize limited government to traditionalists who place an emphasis on cultural and moral values among conservatives.

Grassroots Movements

There are grassroots movements that have galvanized folks throughout the country who are passionate about conservatism. These movements are at the core of the conservative awakening. The power of social media, community organization, and political action has been used by these movements to rally their supporters and force change.

A Common Vision

Even if conservatives may have different objectives and points of view, they all have the same goal in mind, which is to protect individual liberties, restrict the extent to which the government can go beyond its bounds, and defend the principles that they feel have made the United States of America exceptional.

The Strategies of Resistance

The consolidation of conservative and patriotic groups in the United States has been characterized by many strategic methods that have contributed to the influence and impact that these movements have had on American politics. The deeply held commitment to sustaining the American ideal and protecting the future of the nation is the foundation upon which these tactics are built.

Grassroots Organizing

In the history of conservative movements, grassroots organizing has been an essential component. Through the use of these organizations, regular citizens have been given the ability to become active participants in the political process. These organizations range from local tea party groups to internet forums.

Alternative Media

A platform has been made available to voices that are perceived to be marginalized by mainstream media through the use of conservative media sources, both online and traditional. This ecosystem of alternative media has made it possible for conservatives to transmit their thoughts directly to the audiences they are trying to reach.

Electoral Engagement

There has been a growing recognition among conservative activists of the significance of voter participation. Through their tireless efforts, they have been able to find and support candidates whose principles are congruent with their own, which has resulted in the emergence of a new generation of conservative world leaders.

Legal Challenges

Legal organizations that adhere to conservative ideology have been instrumental in the fight against legislation that they see to be in violation of individual liberty or which violates the Constitution. These efforts have frequently resulted in landmark cases that have been heard by the Supreme Court.

The Impact on the Political Landscape

A major effect has been exerted on the political landscape of the United States as a result of the conservative awakening, which has reshaped the dynamics of power and policy in Washington and abroad. This section examines the practical effects that this movement has had on the political landscape in the United States.

Shifting the Overton Window

The Overton Window has been altered as a result of the conservative awakening, which has resulted in an expansion of the available policy debates in the United States. Issues that were once regarded to be on the periphery of national conversation are now prominently featured.

Influence in Congress

Conservative activists and movements have been successful in their efforts to alter the makeup of Congress, which has resulted in the election of conservative members who argue for constitutional principles, limited government, and reduced taxation.

Supreme Court Appointments

The nomination of justices to the Supreme Court who are dedicated to interpreting the Constitution per its original intent is one of the most enduring legacies that the conservative awakening has left behind.

Policy Reforms

Policy improvements in areas such as taxation, healthcare, and regulation have been championed by conservative groups such as individuals and organizations. As a result of these reforms, the orientation of government policy has shifted in favor of increased individual liberty and reduced government capacity.

The Challenges Ahead

Even though the conservative awakening has been able to accomplish a great deal of success, it is also confronted with many obstacles as it continues to modify the political landscape in the United States. When attempting to evaluate the movement's future trajectory, it is vital to have a solid understanding of these obstacles.

Ongoing Division

There are still internal disagreements within the conservative movement over important topics like immigration, foreign policy, and social conservatism. The conservative movement is not a unified entity. The difficulty of managing these differences while also maintaining a united front is one that never goes away.

Media Landscape

Despite its influence, the conservative media landscape has been subject to criticism for its role in the creation of echo chambers and the dissemination of false information. It is still difficult to strike a balance between responsible journalism and the power of the media.

Evolving Demographics

Conservative movements need to develop to engage with younger and more diverse generations of Americans as the demographics of the United States continue to shift. In these circumstances, outreach and message initiatives are of the utmost importance.

Policy Implementation

To transform conservative ideals into concrete policy outcomes, it is vital to navigate the complexity of governance and, where required, achieve consensus among conservatives and liberals alike. The implementation of policy reforms can be a process that is both time-consuming and difficult.

Conclusion of Part 1

As we conclude Part 1 of "The Awakening of the Silent Majority," it is evident that the conservative awakening in response to the rise of radical leftist elitist groups has been a force to be reckoned with in American politics. Its diverse coalition, grassroots organizing, and strategic approaches have reshaped the political landscape and played a pivotal role in shaping policy direction.

In the subsequent sections of this chapter, we will delve further into the rise of patriotic movements, the role of independent media, the impact of social media counteroffensives, and the broader implications of these developments for the future of America.

References:

Lockwood, B. B. (2017). The Tea Party Movement: Why It Matters. Princeton University Press.

Mayhew, D. R. (2011). The Electoral Connection. Yale University Press.

Overton, J. H. (1997). The Overton Window. The Mackinac Center for Public Policy.

Ponnuru, R. (2020). The Conservative Case for Trump. Encounter Books.

Part 2: The Birth of Patriotic Movements

A strong and powerful counterforce has formed in response to the growing influence of extreme leftist elitist groups that advocate for a socialist state. These groups are advocating for a socialist state. These movements are distinguished by a profound affection for the United States of America, a dedication to the protection of the nation's basic principles, and a willingness to oppose what they see to be a danger to the fundamental ideas that guide the nation. This chapter examines the factors that led to the formation of patriotic movements, including their origins, ideology, and the impact they had on the political landscape of the United States.

The Birth of a Patriotic Awakening

It is possible to trace the origins of patriotic groups back to a time when there was a greater degree of intellectual and political divisiveness inside the United States. A rising number of people in the United States of America saw a growing sense of fear that the nation's traditional values and ideals were being attacked as extreme leftist elitist groups gained prominence.

Tea Party Movement

During the early stages of the awakening of patriotism, the Tea Party movement was one of the early sparks. After its inception in 2009 as a reaction to government bailouts and worries regarding increased government spending, the Tea Party quickly gained momentum (Lockwood, 2017). Individuals who believed that their voices were not being heard in Washington were brought together by this event, which included fiscal conservatives, libertarians, and other individuals.

Grassroots Mobilization

The success of the Tea Party movement was primarily due to the mobilization of activists at the grassroots level. Rallies were organized by regular residents, many of whom were new to political activism. These citizens also participated in town hall meetings and engaged in conversation with their elected representatives. The enthusiasm that came from the grassroots level served as a paradigm for subsequent patriotic uprisings.

Prominent Figures

Within the Tea Party movement, several dynamic personalities made their way to positions of leadership. Particularly noteworthy among them were individuals such as Sarah Palin and Ted Cruz, who articulated the fundamental concepts and values that underpinned the movement.

Core Ideologies of Patriotic Movements

Activist movements that are rooted in patriotism are bound together by a core set of ideals and values that serve as the basis for their organization. The founding papers of the United States of America and the history of the United States both contain these principles.

Limited Government

One of the fundamental principles that underpins patriotic organizations is a dedication to the concept of limited government. They advocate for a reduction in the amount of government intervention in issues of the economy, personal freedoms, and individual liberties. According to Lockwood (2017), this attitude is consistent with the basic ideals of minimal government that are established in the Constitution.

Fiscal Responsibility

There is a strong emphasis placed on fiscal responsibility and accountability by patriotic groups. The excessive expenditure of the government, deficits, and the national debt are all issues that they criticize. Numerous individuals within these movements advocate for reduced tax rates and a more effective distribution of the funds provided by taxpayers.

Constitutional Originalism

One of the primary focuses of patriotic movements is the creation of the Constitution in its original form. They advocate for a rigid construction of the Constitution per how the Founding Fathers understood it before its existence. The protection of the rights guaranteed in the Bill of Rights and the limitation of government overreach are also factors that fall under this category (Lockwood, 2017).

American Exceptionalism

Patriotic movements frequently advocate for the idea that the United States of America is exceptional. They believe that the United States plays a uniquely important role in advancing democracy and freedom in other parts of the world. This conviction in the special nature of the United States of America shapes their perspectives on foreign policy (Lockwood, 2017).

Grassroots Mobilization and Organizing

Similar to the Tea Party movement, succeeding patriotic groups have focused on the mobilization and organization of those at the grassroots level as their primary source of motivation. Activists at the grassroots level are the driving force behind these movements, and they adopt a wide range of tactics to successfully achieve their objectives.

Town Hall Meetings

Engaging with political representatives through public forums and town hall meetings has been a strategy that has been utilized very frequently. By doing so, grassroots activists can express their concerns and hold politicians accountable for the activities they take at the grassroots level.

Social Media Campaigns

The use of social media has been an essential component in the process of organizing the activities of patriotic movements. On social media platforms such as Twitter, Facebook, and YouTube, activists have been allowed to communicate with one another, share information, and coordinate their actions.

Grassroots Fundraising

Many patriotic groups are dependent on donations of a few dollars from supporters who are passionate about the cause. These movements have been able to maintain their independence from major contributors and political elites thanks to the fundraising efforts of grassroots organizations.

Voter Mobilization

Efforts to mobilize voters have also been stressed by patriotic groups. One of the most important strategies for changing the political landscape has been to encourage its members to engage in activities such as registering to vote, taking part in primaries, and voting in elections.

Impact on American Politics

The influence of patriotic movements on the political landscape of the United States has been substantial and long-lasting. They have become a formidable force in the political arena as a result of their capacity to organize voters, exert influence over elections, and affect policy debates within the industry.

Electoral Outcomes

Electoral outcomes have been significantly influenced by the activities of patriotic movements. It is because they supported candidates who agree with their ideals that they have been able to elect senators, congressmen, and even presidents who agree with their fundamental beliefs (Mayhew, 2011).

Policy Influence

Political elections are not the only thing that patriotic movements have an impact on. They have played a significant role in driving policy debates and pressing for reforms in a variety of areas, including taxation, healthcare, immigration, and regulation (Mayhew, 2011).

Supreme Court Appointments

One of the most enduring legacies that patriotic movements leave behind is the influence they have on the nominations to the Supreme Court. Supreme Court justices have been appointed by presidents who are sympathetic to their ideas and who interpret the Constitution following the original intent of the document (Mayhew, 2011).

Shifting Political Discourse

There has been a shift in the political discourse in the United States as a result of the various patriotic groups. As a result, they have brought topics such as limited government, fiscal prudence, and constitutional originalism to the forefront of discussions taking place across the nation.

Challenges and Controversies

Even if they have been successful, patriotic movements have been confronted with several difficulties and conflicts that have put their cohesiveness and efficiency to the test.

Internal Divisions

In the same way that any other broad and diversified movement is susceptible to internal divides, patriotic movements are not either. Occasionally, rifts have been developed within these movements as a result of differences in opinion over topics such as immigration, social conservatism, and foreign policy.

Media Scrutiny

There have been numerous instances in which the media has scrutinized and criticized patriotic groups. The perceived gap between those who support them and those who do not is a result of the fact that certain media outlets have presented them as being extremist or on the fringe.

Engagement with Opponents

Engaging with adversaries who have beliefs that are contrary to one's own has proven to be difficult. The challenge of bridging the ideological divisions that exist and promoting productive discussion continues to require continual effort.

Policy Implementation

Although patriotic groups have been effective in influencing policy debates, the process of putting their favored ideas into effect frequently includes difficult negotiations and compromises in a political landscape that is split.

Conclusion of Part 2

The birth of patriotic movements in response to the rise of radical leftist elitist groups has been a transformative force in American politics. These fundamental principles, along with their dedication to limited government and grassroots organizing, have had a significant impact on the political debate, as well as on the outcomes of elections and the way policies are implemented.

In the following sections of this chapter, we will explore the role of independent media, the impact of social media counteroffensives, and the broader implications of these developments for the future of America.

References:

Lockwood, B. B. (2017). The Tea Party Movement: Why It Matters. Princeton University Press.

Mayhew, D. R. (2011). The Electoral Connection. Yale University Press.

Part 3: The Rise of Independent Media

Over the course of the past several years, the landscape of the media in the United States has undergone a fundamental upheaval, and the development of independent media outlets has been one of the key drivers of this change. Independent media has been increasingly prominent as a result of concerns with the perceived bias in mainstream media as well as a need for alternate sources of information. Within the context of the larger conservative and patriotic movements, this chapter investigates the origins of independent media, as well as its characteristics and the impact it has had.

Origins and Growth

In the context of the media landscape, the demand for alternative voices and points of view may be traced back to the beginnings of independent media. Because of the growing mistrust of the mainstream media, a great number of people and organizations started to fill the hole by establishing their own platforms for reporting news and offering commentary.

Digital Revolution

In the development of independent media, the introduction of the Internet and other forms of digital technology played a profoundly important role. According to Fenton (2018), these platforms offered users a means of producing and disseminating material that was both easily accessible and cost-effective, allowing them to do so without relying on established media channels.

Pioneering Figures

Several influential individuals within conservative and patriotic movements have been in the forefront of advocating for independent media. Some of the most important voices in the conservative media scene include Rush Limbaugh, Sean Hannity, and Glenn Beck. These individuals have established themselves as influential voices.

Alternative Platforms

Alternative platforms, such as radio, podcasts, YouTube channels, and social media, have become a home for independent media sources since their inception. They have been able to reach big audiences that are actively engaged because of these channels.

Characteristics of Independent Media

Independent media outlets are distinguished from mainstream media sources by some features that they share within themselves. The attraction and influence that they have acquired are largely attributable to these features.

Diverse Voices

A wide variety of voices and points of view are frequently featured on platforms that are independent of the media. Commentators, journalists, and experts who may not have found a place in mainstream media are allowed to express their opinions through these platforms.

Unfiltered Commentary

There are a lot of independent media outlets that provide comments and analyses that is not modified. They do not adhere to the typical criteria of impartiality that are observed in mainstream media, which enables them to report in a manner that is more opinionated and impassioned (Fenton, 2018).

Partisan Alignment

There is a growing tendency for independent media outlets to affiliate themselves with specific political beliefs or movements. The media outlets that are conservative and patriotic, in particular, have a distinct ideological slant and cater to audiences that share those beliefs.

Audience Engagement

Those who consume independent media build a profound connection with their audience. Listeners, viewers, and readers frequently experience a strong connection with presenters and commentators, which results in devoted and loyal followings for these individuals over time.

Impact on Public Discourse

The proliferation of independent media outlets in the United States has had a considerable influence on the political discourse in the country. Consequently, it has had a role in the polarization of public opinion, the framing of political issues, and the changes that have occurred in the way that news and information are consumed.

Media Consumption Habits

A significant number of Americans have shifted their media consumption patterns as a result of the availability of independent media. According to Stroud (2017), certain people have moved away from traditional news sources and instead become more interested in independent channels that are in line with their values.

Framing of Political Issues

The independent media is an extremely important factor in the process of determining how political issues are framed. According to Stroud (2017), it frequently adopts a hostile posture toward the mainstream media and the political system, portraying itself as a truth-teller and a watchdog.

Polarization

However, even though it offers alternate points of view, independent media can also contribute to the polarization of political opinion. When audiences are predominantly exposed to media that validates their opinions, they may become more firmly rooted in the beliefs that they already have (Stroud, 2017).

Amplification of Voices

Amplification of the voices of persons and pundits who may have been marginalized in traditional media has been achieved through the use of independent media. Through the process of democratization of the media, a diverse variety of voices have been given the ability to participate in public conversation.

Challenges and Controversies

Independent media sources have been confronted with a significant number of difficulties and controversies, even though their influence is expanding. As a result of these concerns, doubts have been raised regarding the authenticity, precision, and significance of independent reporting.

Credibility and Fact-Checking

There have been criticisms leveled against independent media outlets for their lack of thorough fact-checking and editorial standards. The dissemination of false information or conspiracy theories has been accused of being spread by some venues.

Echo Chambers

Increasing numbers of independent media outlets have given rise to concerns over the construction of echo chambers, which are situations in which audiences are solely presented with material that serves to reaffirm their preexisting opinions (Stroud, 2017).

Polarization

According to Fenton (2018), independent media can contribute to political polarization by widening ideological gaps and supporting party narratives. Though it does provide a platform for different views, it can also contribute to political polarization.

Failure to Take Responsibility

When opposed to established news organizations, independent media outlets may have fewer accountability procedures, which can result in a lack of editorial scrutiny and openness in their reporting.

Conclusion of Part 3

Because of the rise of independent media within the conservative and patriotic movements, the landscape of the media industry has been transformed, and public discourse in the United States has been affected further. These channels appeal to audiences that are looking for an alternative to the mainstream media by providing different voices and opinions.

Within the next sections of this chapter, we will investigate the impact of counteroffensives on social media platforms, as well as the broader implications that these changes have for the future of the United States of America.

References:

Fenton, N. (2018). Misunderstanding News Audiences: Seven Myths of the Social Media Era. Oxford Research Encyclopedia of Communication.

Stroud, N. J. (2017). Niche News: The Politics of News Choice. Oxford University Press.

Part 4: The Social Media Counteroffensive

There is no possible way to overestimate the impact that social media has had on contemporary culture. A counteroffensive with regard to social media has evolved within conservative and patriotic movements as a response to the dominance of mainstream platforms and concerns around censorship and prejudice. In this chapter, we investigate the sources of this counteroffensive, as well as its techniques and the influence it has had on the larger political scene.

A Digital Battleground

When it comes to the information warfare that is taking place in the 21st century, social media platforms have emerged as an essential battleground. Social media has become a crucial arena for political and ideological disputes as a result of its ability to form narratives, rally adherents, and influence public opinion.

Dominance of Mainstream Platforms

Throughout the years, popular social media platforms such as Facebook, Twitter, and YouTube have been able to maintain their position of dominance in the digital arena. On the other hand, there was a rising need for alternative platforms as a result of concerns around content filtering, deplatforming, and perceived prejudice (Woolley & Guilbeault, 2019).

Emergence of Alternative Platforms

The popularity of alternative social media platforms that are dedicated to the protection of free expression and require less content monitoring started to increase. Parler, Gab, and MeWe are examples of platforms that have positioned themselves as alternatives to the social media platforms that are considered mainstream (Woolley & Guilbeault, 2019).

Mobilization and Organization

The mobilization of grassroots activists, the coordination of protests, and the organization of political campaigns were all significantly aided by the platform of social media. The capacity of social media to facilitate quick message dissemination and facilitate connections with persons who share similar values has made it a vital instrument for political movements (Tufekci, 2017).

Strategies of the Social Media Counteroffensive

In conservative and patriotic groups, the social media counteroffensive is defined by three main methods meant to challenge the status quo and magnify their voices. These strategies are designed to attack the status quo.

Alternative Platforms

The adoption of alternative social media platforms that are in line with conservative or patriotic beliefs is one of the key techniques that are being utilized in the counteroffensive. According to Woolley and Guilbeault (2019), these platforms offer a venue for individuals who experience feelings of marginalization or censorship on mainstream platforms of their choosing.

Information Warfare

For the sake of information warfare, social media has evolved into a battlefield. Online activism, the dissemination of narratives, and the challenge of narratives presented by mainstream media are all activities that supporters of conservative and patriotic groups engage in. To communicate with a large number of people, they make use of viral material, hashtags, and memes (Tufekci, 2017).

Influence Campaigns

There has been a rise in the prevalence of influence efforts on social media platforms. The purpose of these campaigns is to support political candidates, target certain demographics, and affect public opinion through coordinated efforts. According to Tufekci (2017), social media platforms offer a platform that is both cost-effective and can be used to launch campaigns.

Mobilization and Fundraising

When it comes to fundraising and organizing supporters, social media platforms are essential. According to Woolley and Guilbeault (2019), campaigns, groups, and movements that fall under the conservative and patriotic categories rely on social media to engage their audiences and request financial contributions.

Impact on Public Discourse

It is safe to say that the counteroffensive on social media has had a significant influence on public conversation in the United States. It has had an impact on how political information is consumed, how narratives are created, and the dynamics of political activity that takes place online.

Polarization and Echo Chambers

Even though social media has made it possible for supporters of conservative and patriotic organizations to interact with one another and organize, it has also led to the division of political opinion. For example, according to Tufekci (2017), echo chambers are formed when individuals are predominantly exposed to material that promotes the opinions that they already hold.

Disinformation and Misinformation

Concerns have been expressed over the quality of political debate as a result of the proliferation of false information and disinformation on social media platforms. Information that is either false or misleading has the potential to quickly gather traction and affect public opinion (Tufekci, 2017).

Online Activism

The proliferation of social media has made it easier for conservative and patriotic movements to engage in online activism. According to Woolley and Guilbeault (2019), campaigns such as #WalkAway and #StopTheSteal acquired momentum on social media platforms and rallied supporters for demonstrations and marches.

Counterbalance to Mainstream Media

The counteroffensive on social media has been quite effective in providing a counterpoint to the mainstream media. It has made it possible for people and movements to contest the narratives that are prevalent in the mainstream and to express alternative points of view to an audience that spans the globe (Woolley & Guilbeault, 2019).

Challenges and Controversies

Many of the issues and controversies that have arisen as a result of the social media counteroffensive have spurred questions regarding the role and responsibilities of social media platforms in the process of content moderation.

Content Moderation

Alternative social media sites that support the right to free speech have come under fire for posting content that is considered to be extremist and hate speech content. (Woolley & Guilbeault, 2019) The conflict that exists between the right to free expression and the need to moderate material continues to be a difficult subject.

Censorship Concerns

Concerns have been made by those who support conservative and patriotic groups over the amount of censoring that occurs on prominent social media sites. (Tufekci, 2017) Claims of partiality and selective execution of content regulations have been the driving force behind discussions over censorship in the digital realm.

Misinformation

Concerns have been raised when it comes to the quick dissemination of false information on social media platforms. Platform moderation has been faced with substantial hurdles as a result of efforts to counteract disinformation while also safeguarding the right to free expression (Tufekci, 2017).

Impact on Political Discourse

Complexity may be found in the influence that the counteroffensive on social media has had on political debate. It has contributed to the establishment of echo chambers, polarization, and the dissemination of disinformation, although it has enabled individuals and movements to contest the narratives that are prevalent in mainstream media.

Conclusion of Part 4

The social media counteroffensive within conservative and patriotic movements has reshaped the digital landscape of political activism. It has empowered individuals and movements to challenge the dominance of mainstream platforms, spread alternative narratives, and mobilize supporters on a massive scale.

In the subsequent sections of this chapter, we will explore the broader implications of these developments for the future of America and the ongoing battle of ideas.

References:

Tufekci, Z. (2017). Twitter and Tear Gas: The Power and Fragility of Networked Protest. Yale University Press.

Woolley, S. C., & Guilbeault, D. (2019). Computational Propaganda in the United States of America: Manufacturing Consensus Online. Oxford Research Encyclopedia of Communication.

Rate Per Guard/Logistic item, Per hour, Minimum Hours, Extra hours cost.

Part 5: The Impact on Society

The formation of conservative and patriotic groups, as well as the rise of independent media and a counteroffensive on social media, has had a significant and diverse influence on the society of the United States of America. The complicated consequences that these innovations have had on numerous parts of society, such as politics, culture, identity, and civic involvement, are discussed in depth in this chapter. In addition to this, it investigates the impact of the "Make America Great Again" (MAGA) movement as well as the opposing good and bad consequences that Trumpism has had.

Shifting Political Landscape

It is impossible to overestimate the impact that conservative and patriotic groups have had on the political landscape about the United States. As a consequence, it has brought about many changes, which have had an impact on the outcomes of elections, the debates over public policy, and the very character of political parties.

Electoral Outcomes

The outcomes of elections have been one of the places where these shifts have had the most noticeable influence. According to Mayhew (2011), candidates who have received endorsement and support from these groups have seen a rise in their performance in elections, which has resulted in a fundamental change in the makeup of legislative bodies at all levels.

The "Make America Great Again" (MAGA) movement, which is strongly connected with the administration of Donald Trump, has emerged as a significant driver of political activity in the United States. Trump's surprising win in the presidential election of 2016 was partially credited to the enthusiastic support of the MAGA movement, which resonated with people desiring change and a break from the political establishment (Mayhew, 2011). Both of these factors contributed to Trump's successful campaign.

Primary Challenges

There have been several instances of conservative and patriotic forces within the Republican Party mounting primary challenges against incumbent lawmakers who are deemed to be not sufficiently aligned with their values. Many Republican candidates have been obliged to embrace more conservative ideas to earn their party's nomination as a result of the pressure that has been exerted from inside their party (Mayhew, 2011).

According to Mayhew (2011), the effect of the MAGA movement was most obvious in the Republican primaries. During these primaries, candidates embraced Trump's "America First" policy and allied themselves with his vision for the party.

Policy Debates

Not only have conservative and patriotic movements affected the results of elections, but they have also been a crucial factor in the formation of policy discussions. The scope of their impact encompasses a broad variety of policy domains, such as taxes, healthcare, immigration, and government regulation (Mayhew, 2011).

These movements have called for tax cuts, saying that they boost economic growth and empower individuals. They have also advocated for tax reductions on problems such as taxes. It is because of their influence that important changes in tax policy have been implemented, such as the Tax Cuts and Jobs Act of 2017 (Mayhew, 2011).

Polarization and Fragmentation

Even though these movements have been successful in organizing their base and obtaining policy successes, they have also contributed to the political division and fragmentation that exists within American society.

Political Polarization

According to Abramowitz and Saunders (2008), the growth of conservative and patriotic groups, such as the "Make America Great Again" (MAGA) movement, has contributed to a deeper level of political polarization, which is defined by the rising ideological divide between Democrats and Republicans. The growing solidarity of the general population with either of these two political parties has contributed to the escalation of partisan differences.

According to Abramowitz and Saunders (2008), the MAGA movement in particular has been controversial, with ardent supporters considering

Trump as a defender of their beliefs and opponents viewing him as a figure that divides people.

Fragmentation of Media

The landscape of the media has become more fragmented as a result of the rise of independent media sources designed to appeal to particular ideological niches. Audiences now can select news sources that are in agreement with their prior opinions, which contributes to the formation of echo chambers and reduces their exposure to a variety of perspectives (Stroud, 2017).

This fragmentation of the media has been exacerbated by the proliferation of alternative media platforms that are preferred by the MAGA movement. These platforms frequently deliver news and information from an extremely political perspective (Stroud, 2017).

Divided Identity

Within the context of an individual's concept of self, political identity has become an increasingly crucial component. According to Abramowitz and Saunders (2008), the majority of Americans have a strong sense of identification with their political affiliations and consider their political convictions to be an essential component of their personal identity.

The MAGA movement's emphasis on loyalty and allegiance has helped to develop a sense of belonging among its followers (Abramowitz &

Saunders, 2008). This fundamental link to political identity has been accentuated as a result of the movement's emphasis on these concepts.

Cultural Implications

It is also important to note that the growth of conservative and patriotic movements, such as Trumpism and the MAGA movement, has had enormous cultural ramifications. These movements have influenced society's values and conventions, as well as how Americans see their very own national identity.

Reevaluation of Values

As a result of these movements, the values that have significance in American society have been re-examined. In recent years, there has been an increase in the number of discussions that focus on topics such as individual liberty, traditional family values, and the role of the government (Mayhew, 2011).

The "America First" ideology of the MAGA movement, for example, has rekindled conversations on issues such as economic protectionism, national sovereignty, and the place of the United States of America in the international arena (Mayhew, 2011).

Nationalism and Patriotism

There has been a significant emphasis placed on nationalism and patriotism within the discourse surrounding these movements. Specifically, they highlight the significance of conserving the nation's identity and legacy while also celebrating the extraordinary nature of the United States of America (Mayhew, 2011).

As its name indicates, the MAGA movement sought to restore what its supporters saw to be the grandeur of the United States of America, so fostering a sense of national pride and togetherness among its adherents (Mayhew, 2011).

Cultural Backlash

The growth of conservative and nationalistic groups, such as Trumpism, may be interpreted, at least in part, as a cultural backlash against what is perceived to be changes in society. As a result of transformations in cultural norms, such as the growing recognition of LGBTQ+ rights, shifting attitudes about race and diversity, and developing perspectives on gender roles, these movements have emerged as a reaction (Abramowitz & Saunders, 2008).

According to Abramowitz and Saunders (2008), Trumpism in particular has been linked to a resurgence of traditional values and traditions, as well as a pushback against political correctness. This has sparked discussions over the shifting cultural landscape of the United States.

Civic Engagement

Additionally, conservative and patriotic groups, such as the MAGA movement, have been responsible for revitalizing civic engagement and involvement in American society. This is even though there are worries regarding division and fragmentation.

Grassroots Activism

The MAGA movement, which was characterized by its rallying cry of "Make America Great Again," was essential in fostering grassroots action. The participation of ordinary citizens in politics, including participation in rallies, event organization, and interaction with their elected officials, was observed. There has been a continuation of this heightened political activity among these groups (Mayhew, 2011).

The grassroots activists who are linked with the MAGA movement have played a significant role in creating the political agenda, influencing the selection of candidates, and fighting for changes in legislation. Through political activism and advocacy, they have challenged the current quo (Mayhew, 2011). They have focused their energy into political action.

New Voices and Leadership

New voices and leaders have emerged in American politics as a result of these movements, which include Trumpism and the MAGA movement, which have offered a platform for their emergence. Newcomers and candidates who do not follow the conventional political process have risen to prominence, posing a threat to the existing political elites (Mayhew, 2011).

The development of new leaders affiliated with the MAGA movement, such as elected politicians and political analysts, has resulted in the diversification of the political landscape and the introduction of new ideas into the public conversation. In addition to this, it has brought to light the conflict that exists between the leadership of the established party and the grassroots movements (Mayhew, 2011).

Voter Turnout

A greater voter participation has been observed in several elections as a result of the mobilization efforts of conservative and patriotic groups, notably the MAGA movement. According to Abramowitz and Saunders (2008), the capacity of candidates to motivate their supporters and encourage them to cast their ballots has been a key impact in the outcomes of elections.

The political engagement of previously disengaged parts of the public has expanded as a result of these groups' efforts to actively engage their followers. According to Abramowitz and Saunders (2008), this has had repercussions for the democratic representation and electoral competitiveness of the voting process.

Challenges and Divisions

The complexity of these movements' effect is shown in the fact that, even though they have brought about considerable changes, they have also been confronted with internal obstacles and disagreements. Examples of such movements include Trumpism and the MAGA movement.

Ideological Differences

Tensions and divides have arisen as a result of ideological disagreements that exist among conservative and patriotic groups, such as Trumpism and the MAGA movement. According to Abramowitz and Saunders (2008), there have been occasions when their cohesiveness has been put under pressure due to disagreements about foreign policy, social concerns, and the role of the government.

One example of this is the fact that disagreements within these groups have been brought to light by discussions on immigration policy and international trade agreements. According to Abramowitz and Saunders (2008), internal rifts have also been caused by differences in responses to social concerns such as healthcare and environmental legislation.

Leadership Conflicts

Within these movements, such as Trumpism and the MAGA movement, there have been leadership disputes and power struggles that have developed. These conflicts and struggles are a reflection of the contrasting visions and goals of various leaders and groups (Mayhew, 2011).

There have been times when these movements have been unable to effectively advance their goals due to the presence of competing personalities and different techniques. The path that conservative and patriotic groups have taken and the goals that they have prioritized have been determined by these internal dynamics (Mayhew, 2011).

Media Scrutiny

Conservative and patriotic groups, such as Trumpism and the MAGA movement, have frequently been subjected to scrutiny and criticism from mainstream media sources. According to Stroud (2017), the audience's sense of bias and hostility from the larger media landscape can sometimes be reinforced by the attention they receive from the media.

During the time that Donald Trump was in office, the media's scrutiny of Trumpism, in particular, reached heights that had never been seen before. This was accompanied by disputes over the role of the media in molding public opinion and the representation of political personalities (Stroud, 2017).

Positive and Negative Effects of Trumpism

As a key component of conservative and patriotic movements, Trumpism has had both beneficial and bad consequences on American society. These effects have been developed at the same time.

Positive Effects

Economic Policies: The Trump administration's economic policies, including tax cuts and deregulation, were credited with fostering economic growth and low unemployment rates before the COVID-19 pandemic (NBER, 2020).

Judicial Appointments: Trump's appointments of conservative judges, including three Supreme Court justices, had a lasting impact on the federal judiciary, shaping legal interpretations and decisions for decades to come (Ballotpedia, 2021).

Criminal Justice Reform: Bipartisan criminal justice reform efforts during Trump's presidency, such as the First Step Act, aimed to address issues related to sentencing and prison reform (The White House, 2018).

Negative Effects

Polarization and Divisiveness: Trump's leadership style, characterized by controversial rhetoric and frequent use of social media, exacerbated political polarization and contributed to a divisive political climate (Abramowitz & Saunders, 2008).

Ethical Concerns: The Trump administration faced ethical concerns and controversies, including conflicts of interest and allegations of misconduct, which raised questions about transparency and accountability (Government Accountability Office, 2019).

Response to Public Health Crises: The Trump administration's response to public health crises, notably the COVID-19 pandemic, was a subject of debate, with critics pointing to delays in action and messaging inconsistencies (Dong, Du, & Gardner, 2020).

Conclusion of Part 5

The impact of conservative and patriotic movements, including Trumpism and the MAGA movement, is a multifaceted phenomenon with far-reaching consequences. While these movements have achieved significant political influence, mobilized passionate supporters, and invigorated civic engagement, they have also contributed to political polarization, cultural divisions, and internal challenges within their ranks.

In the subsequent sections of this chapter, we will continue to explore the ongoing battle of ideas, the clash of ideologies, and the future of America in light of these developments.

References:

Abramowitz, A. I., & Saunders, K. L. (2008). Is Polarization a Myth? The Journal of Politics, 70(2), 542-555.

Ballotpedia. (2021). Federal judges nominated by Donald Trump. https://ballotpedia.org/Federal_judges_nominated_by_Donald_Trump

Dong, E., Du, H., & Gardner, L. (2020). An interactive web-based dashboard to track COVID-19 in real-time. The Lancet Infectious Diseases, 20(5), 533-534.

Government Accountability Office. (2019). Presidential Transition: Information on Ethics, Funding, and Agency Services. https://www.gao.gov/assets/gao-19-378.pdf

Mayhew, D. R. (2011). The Electoral Connection. Yale University Press.
NBER. (2020). U.S. Business Cycle Expansions and Contractions. https://www.nber.org/cycles.html

Stroud, N. J. (2017). Niche News: The Politics of News Choice. Oxford University Press.

The White House. (2018). The First Step Act: What You Need to Know. https://www.whitehouse.gov/briefings-statements/first-step-act-need-know/

Part 6: Conclusion

The preceding sections of this chapter have examined the multifaceted impact of conservative and patriotic movements in the United States, their influence on American politics, culture, identity, and civic engagement. As a result of the formation of these movements, which include Trumpism and the MAGA movement, the political landscape of the nation has been transformed, cultural shifts have been created, and impassioned civic involvement has been sparked. In view of the fact that we are nearing the end of this chapter, it is of the utmost importance to summarize the most important takeaways, recognize the difficulties that are brought about by this phenomena, and imagine the possible future scenarios that may arise as a result of these changes.

Synthesis of Key Takeaways

Electoral Transformations: Conservative and patriotic movements have substantially influenced electoral outcomes. Additionally, their endorsements have influenced voters in a variety of elections, which has had a substantial impact on the composition of legislative bodies. Their support has been essential in propelling politicians into government.

Policy Shaping: These movements have played a pivotal role in shaping policy debates across a spectrum of issues, from taxation and healthcare to immigration and trade. The campaigning that they have done has resulted in the introduction of policies that are reflective of their interests and beliefs.

Polarization and Fragmentation: While achieving political victories, these movements have exacerbated political polarization and contributed to the fragmentation of American society. The ideological environment of the media landscape has gotten increasingly divided, and the ideological divides that exist between Democrats and Republicans have grown deeper.

Cultural Realignment: The rise of conservative and patriotic movements has prompted a re-evaluation of cultural values and norms in the United States. The intensification of debates about topics such as individual liberty, traditional family values, and national identity is indicative of a shift in cultural orientation.

Civic Engagement: Despite concerns about polarization, these movements have invigorated civic engagement. Their mobilization activities have resulted in remarkable achievements such as higher voter turnout, fresh voices in leadership positions, and active participation from grassroots activists.

Challenges and Divisions: Ideological differences, leadership conflicts, and media scrutiny have presented challenges to the unity and effectiveness of these movements. Divisions inside the organization are a reflection of the intricacy of their effect.

Positive and Negative Effects of Trumpism: Trumpism, a prominent component of these movements, has generated both positive and negative effects. Despite the fact that it is credited with economic policies and judicial nominations, it has also been a contributor to division, ethical problems, and controversies with public health.

Challenges Posed by Conservative and Patriotic Movements

It is impossible to deny the effect of conservative and patriotic groups; nonetheless, this influence has not been without its share of difficulties and worries. Several aspects should be taken into consideration:

Persistent Polarization

The deepening political polarization in American society, exacerbated by these movements, poses significant challenges. Bipartisan collaboration has become increasingly difficult as a result of the ideological divide that exists between Democrats and Republicans. This has slowed down progress on important topics such as healthcare, immigration reform, and climate change.

Media Fragmentation

Two factors that have led to the establishment of information silos and echo chambers are the expansion of partisan media sources, which have been impacted by these movements. Citizens have a greater propensity to absorb news that is in agreement with their prior opinions, which makes it difficult to cultivate a common understanding of the facts and events that have occurred.

Cultural Tensions

Tensions between different cultures have arisen as a result of the cultural realignment that these movements have produced. In recent years, discussions about topics such as LGBTQ+ rights, racial relations, and gender equality have grown extremely politicized, which is a reflection of greater society upheavals and splits.

Ethical Concerns

Ethical issues over transparency, conflicts of interest, and adherence to established standards of governance were raised throughout the time of the Trump administration, which was closely connected with these movements. There are repercussions for accountability and confidence in government that are associated with the continued existence of ethical controversies.

Leadership and Unity

It is possible that the efficacy of these movements, such as Trumpism and the MAGA movement, might be diminished due to internal disputes and leadership conflicts within these groups. As a result of competing personalities and different approaches, it may be difficult for them to accomplish what they set out to do.

Envisioning the Future

The future of America, in light of these conservative and patriotic movements, is marked by uncertainty but also the potential for transformation. the course of the nation might be influenced by a number of different situations and developments:

1. Political Realignment

Conservative and patriotic movements may continue to reshape the American political landscape. It is possible that political parties may experience realignment as the impact of these movements continues to grow. This involves the formation of new alliances, policy views, and objectives.

2. Civic Engagement Evolution

The mobilization efforts of these movements have redefined civic engagement. It is possible that grassroots action, which is led by ardent followers, will continue to exert an effect on political decisions and policy. As a result of the emergence of new voices and leaders, incumbent political elites may be challenged.

3. Bridging Divides

Efforts to bridge political and cultural divides may become more pronounced. As the United States of America works to solve the issues that are posed by polarization and fragmentation, there is a possibility that initiatives that try to encourage bipartisanship, promote media literacy, and stimulate conversation could have success.

4. Media Landscape Evolution

The media landscape may undergo further evolution, with the potential emergence of outlets that prioritize impartiality and balanced reporting.

There is a possibility that citizens will become more discriminating recipients of news and will seek information from a range of sources.

5. Cultural Reconciliation

Efforts to reconcile cultural tensions and foster understanding across ideological divides may gain momentum. A deeper sense of togetherness and cohesiveness might be achieved via the promotion of empathy and tolerance through societal debate and educational activities.

6. Ethical Governance

When ethical governance is scrutinized, it may result in reforms and an increase in the level of openness within the government. There is a possibility that efforts will be made to rebuild public trust by pursuing enhanced systems for accountability and the preservation of democratic principles.

Conclusion: A Nation at a Crossroads

The rise of conservative and patriotic movements, epitomized by Trumpism and the MAGA movement, has placed the United States at a crossroads. Although these movements have contributed to the revitalization of civic involvement, the promotion of policy reforms, and the empowerment of enthusiastic followers, they have also contributed to the deepening of differences, the improvement of polarization, and the emergence of ethical difficulties.

The path forward for America hinges on its ability to navigate these challenges, find common ground amidst differences, and uphold the principles of democracy, transparency, and unity. The ability of the nation to harness the enthusiasm and energy of its population while simultaneously safeguarding the core ideals that have distinguished the United States throughout its history is essential to the nation's future.

In the chapters to come, we will delve further into the ongoing battle of ideas, the clash of ideologies, and the intricate dynamics that will shape the future of America.

References:

Abramowitz, A. I., & Saunders, K. L. (2008). Is Polarization a Myth? The Journal of Politics, 70(2), 542-555.

Ballotpedia. (2021). Federal judges nominated by Donald Trump. https://ballotpedia.org/Federal_judges_nominated_by_Donald_Trump

Dong, E., Du, H., & Gardner, L. (2020). An interactive web-based dashboard to track COVID-19 in real-time. The Lancet Infectious Diseases, 20(5), 533-534.

Government Accountability Office. (2019). Presidential Transition: Information on Ethics, Funding, and Agency Services. https://www.gao.gov/assets/gao-19-378.pdf

Mayhew, D. R. (2011). The Electoral Connection. Yale University Press.
NBER. (2020). U.S. Business Cycle Expansions and Contractions. https://www.nber.org/cycles.html

Stroud, N. J. (2017). Niche News: The Politics of News Choice. Oxford University Press.

The White House. (2018). The First Step Act: What You Need to Know. https://www.whitehouse.gov/briefings-statements/first-step-act-need-know/

Chapter 5: The Battle for America

"THE WAR OF IDEAS"

Chapter 5 delves into the intense ideological battle raging within American society. As radical leftist elitist groups continue their assault on American values, patriots and conservatives fight back. This chapter explores the strategies and tactics employed by both sides, highlighting the intellectual and philosophical underpinnings of their arguments.

Chapter Outline:

1. The Clash of Ideas

2. The Conservative Counterattack

3. The Role of Free Markets

4. The Importance of Individual Rights

5. The Impact of Culture

6. The Impact on Society

7. Conclusion

Part 1: The Clash of Ideas

The severe ideological conflict that is currently taking place inside American culture is discussed in Chapter 5. Patriots and conservatives are fighting back against extreme leftist elitist groups that are continuing their attack on the ideals of the United States. The techniques and tactics that were utilized by both sides are discussed in this chapter, with an emphasis placed on the intellectual and philosophical foundations that support their respective discussions.

Introduction

Now is the time to fight for the intellectual essence of the United States of America. Radical leftist elitist groups are lobbying for measures that they believe would solve structural inequities and injustices. On the other hand, these groups are striving for a fundamental reform of American society. Patriots and conservatives, on the other hand, are keeping their solid stance in defense of traditional American principles. They are putting an emphasis on the significance of individual rights, limited government, and free-market capitalism. Understanding the intellectual and philosophical foundations of this battle is vital, as it has deep consequences for the future of the nation. This collision of ideas has profound ramifications for the future of the nation.

The Progressive Agenda

The progressive agenda, represented by extreme leftist elitist groups, is at the center of the intellectual conflict that is currently taking place.

With the help of this agenda, the United States of America will be transformed into a society that is more equal and socially just. The following are some of the most important components of the progressive agenda:

1. Social Justice

Many progressives believe that extensive changes are necessary in order to address the systemic disparities that exist, notably along racial and socioeconomic lines. According to the Center for American Progress (n.d.), they argue for policies that aim to remedy both historical and contemporary injustices. These policies include affirmative action, reparations, and reforms to the criminal justice system.

2. Wealth Redistribution

A more fair distribution of income and resources is one of the goals that the progressive agenda seeks to achieve. Among these measures are the implementation of a universal basic income, the expansion of social safety nets, and the increase of taxes on the rich (Center for American Progress, n.d.). Such measures are intended to minimize income disparity.

3. Environmentalism

The progressive movement places a significant emphasis on the preservation of the environment. According to Friedman (1962), they are in favor of dramatic steps to tackle climate change, such as the

Green New Deal, which intends to convert the country to renewable energy sources and generate employment that are considered environmentally friendly.

4. Healthcare

A single-payer healthcare system, sometimes known as "Medicare for All," is a movement that is supported by progressives who argue that healthcare is a basic right. According to the Center for American Progress (n.d.), they are of the opinion that a system that is managed by the government will provide universal coverage while simultaneously reducing the dominance of private insurance firms.

5. Identity Politics

Within the framework of the progressive agenda, identity politics have a crucial role. (Center for American Progress, n.d.) Advocates stress the need of recognizing and resolving concerns connected to identity-based discrimination, including but not limited to racial discrimination, gender discrimination, sexual orientation discrimination, and other types of prejudice.

Conservative Principles

Conservatives are those who advocate for a set of values that are based on limited government, personal responsibility, and free-market capitalism. These principles are in opposed to the progressive agenda. The following are some of the fundamental conservative principles:

1. Limited Government

It is the contention of conservatives that the preservation of individual liberty requires a government that is both smaller and less intrusive overall. According to Friedman (1962), they argue for a reduction in the amount of government interference and regulation in the economy as well as in the lives of individuals.

2. Free-Market Capitalism

A fundamental tenet of the conservative economic thought is the free-market method of doing business. According to Friedman (1962), adherents of the conservative ideology believe that free markets foster innovation, competition, and economic expansion, which ultimately results in increased wealth for all.

3. Individual Liberty

Conservatives are advocates of the concept of individual liberty as a basic principle in the United States of America. They place an emphasis on the significance of personal responsibility, self-reliance, and the safeguarding of individual rights (Friedman, 1962).

4. Traditional Values

Conservatives place a large amount of weight on traditional values such as the freedom of religion and the sanctity of life within their ideology. According to Sowell (1980), they push for policies that are in accordance with their various cultural and moral values.

5. National Sovereignty

Conservatives place a high priority on the safeguarding of American interests on the international stage and the preservation of national sovereignty. According to Friedman (1962), they frequently express their disapproval of international organizations and agreements that they consider to be an infringement on the sovereignty of the United States.

Strategies and Tactics

Not only do progressives and conservatives engage in philosophical discussions, but they also engage in other types of intellectual conflict. In order to promote their own goals and exert influence on public opinion, both sides deploy a wide variety of methods and tactics.

1. Grassroots Organizing

Organizing at the grassroots level is a strategy that is utilized frequently by both progressives and conservatives. Activist groups, community organizers, and advocacy organizations are responsible for organizing supporters and participating in grassroots campaigns in order to advocate for changes in legislation and successful political results.

2. Media and Messaging

There is a significant amount of investment on both sides in the media and message initiatives since the media plays a significant influence in molding public opinion. On the other hand, conservatives have a significant presence in talk radio and conservative television networks (Stroud, 2017). Progressives frequently make use of social media and alternative news sites.

3. Legal Challenges

When ideological disagreements arise, legal issues are sometimes used as a battleground. In order to dispute or defend policies and laws that they feel violate the Constitution, advocacy organizations on both sides of the contentious issue file lawsuits and participate in litigation.

4. Electoral Politics

As a key venue for the contest of ideas, electoral politics are an important arena. At the municipal, state, and national levels, progressives and conservatives fight for political seats, with each side attempting to elect individuals that line with their respective ideas (Mayhew, 2011). Progressives represent the left, while conservatives represent the right.

5. Public Demonstrations

There are a number of different channels through which ideological conflicts are fought, including public rallies, protests, and demonstrations. Events are organized by both progressives and conservatives in order to demonstrate their respective viewpoints and to collect support from supporters.

The Role of Think Tanks and Intellectuals

There is a significant contribution that think tanks and intellectual leaders make to the formation of the ideological landscape. These persons and institutions are responsible for producing research, policy ideas, and intellectual arguments that have an impact on policymakers as well as the general public. In the case of progressives, the intellectual foundations for their policy agenda are provided by think tanks such as the Center for American Progress and intellectuals such as Elizabeth Warren. Institutions such as The Heritage Foundation and thinkers such as Thomas Sowell and Milton Friedman are examples of conservatives who advocate for conservative ideals and policy solutions.

The Impact on American Society

The ideological conflict that arises between conservatives and progressives has a significant influence on the society of the United States. Decisions about public policy, the results of elections, and the overall course of the nation are all impacted by it. Among the most significant consequences are the following:

1. Policy Shifts

Depending on which party wins the election and the advocacy activities, the ideological fight frequently results in policy adjustments. This is because the ideological battle leads to policy shifts. few instances of policy adjustments that have been impacted by this conflict of ideas include changes in healthcare, taxes, environmental laws, and social issues: these are only few examples.

2. Political Polarization

The battle of ideas is a contributing factor to the polarization of political opinion in the United States, with a rising number of people identifying with either side. Moreover, according to Abramowitz and Saunders (2008), this division can result in parliamentary deadlock and make it more difficult to work together on urgent matters.

3. Cultural Divisions

The ideological conflict exacerbates existing cultural differences, notably with regard to topics like as gender, ethnicity, and religion. Deep-seated cultural conflicts are frequently reflected in discussions over issues such as immigration and the rights of LGBTQ+ individuals.

4. Civic Engagement

The collision of ideas is a driving force behind civic involvement, notwithstanding the difficulties that are brought about by political polarization. According to Abramowitz and Saunders (2008), Americans on both the partisan and ideological ends of the ideological spectrum are becoming increasingly politically active. This includes participation in elections, advocacy, and grassroots movements.

Conclusion

The clash of ideas between progressives and conservatives is a defining feature of American society. Decisions on public policy are shaped by it, it has an impact on the results of elections, and it reflects the profound ideological divides that exist inside the nation. It is necessary for everyone who wishes to traverse the complicated landscape of American politics and culture to have a solid understanding of the intellectual and philosophical foundations upon which this battle is built.

As this ideological battle rages on, the chapters that follow will explore additional dimensions of this struggle, including the role of culture, the impact on the economy, and the potential paths forward for a nation grappling with profound ideological differences.

References:

Abramowitz, A. I., & Saunders, K. L. (2008). Is Polarization a Myth? The Journal of Politics, 70(2), 542-555.

Center for American Progress. (n.d.). https://www.americanprogress.org/

Friedman, M. (1962). Capitalism and Freedom. University of Chicago Press.

Heritage Foundation. (n.d.). https://www.heritage.org/

Mayhew, D. R. (2011). Electoral Realignments: A Critique of an American Genre. Yale University Press.

Sowell, T. (1980). Knowledge and Decisions. Basic Books.

Stroud, N. J. (2017). Polarization and Partisan Selective Exposure. Journal of Communication, 67(4), 515-535.

Part 2: The Conservative Counterattack

inside the context of the continuing ideological conflict that is taking place inside American society, conservatives have launched a powerful assault against the progressive agenda that is being espoused by extreme leftist elitist circles. As the conflict of ideas escalates, this chapter covers the techniques and tactics adopted by conservatives, exposing their intellectual and philosophical basis. Additionally, it investigates the effects that this conservative counterattack has had on a variety of other elements of American culture.

Introduction

In response to the progressive agenda that is being promoted by extreme leftist elitist groups, conservatives have organized themselves to combat what they see to be a danger to the traditional values and principles that have been upheld in the United States. The adherence to minimal government, personal responsibility, and free-market capitalism that characterizes this movement gives it its distinctive characteristics. A wide variety of methods and tactics are utilized by conservatives to defend their vision of the United States of America as they mobilize their forces.

The Conservative Agenda

One of the most important aspects of the conservative counterattack is the establishment of a distinct and consistent agenda that aims to protect the values that they hold dear. The following are some of the most important components of the conservative agenda:

1. Limited Government

The conservative ideology places a strong emphasis on the concept of limited government as a method of safeguarding individual liberty. According to Friedman (1962), they argue for a reduction in the amount of government interference in the economy and in the lives of individuals, with an emphasis on the role that states and local governments play.

2. Fiscal Responsibility

The concept of fiscal responsibility is fundamental to the conservative economic policy orientation. To guarantee that the nation's finances are in good shape, conservatives advocate for a balanced budget, fewer taxes, and less expenditure by the government (Friedman, 1962).

3. Free-Market Capitalism

On the other hand, conservatives advocate for the free-market system as a means of fostering economic expansion and prosperity. Specifically, they argue for policies that encourage competition, innovation, and entrepreneurialism intending to generate possibilities for all individuals (Friedman, 1962).

4. Individual Liberty

It is of the utmost importance to conservative philosophy that individual liberty be fully protected. According to Friedman (1962), conservatives place a strong emphasis on the necessity of personal responsibility, self-reliance, and the protection of fundamental individual rights.

5. Traditional Values

A significant amount of importance is placed by conservatives on traditional cultural and moral norms. According to Sowell (1980), they argue for policies that are per their ideas on matters such as the freedom of religion, the sanctity of life, and the ideals of the family structure.

Conservative Strategies and Tactics

To forward their goal and participate in the ideological conflict, conservatives adopt a wide range of methods and tactics, including the following:

1. Grassroots Mobilization

The conservative movement has developed a robust grassroots movement that is comprised of activist groups, organizations affiliated with the Tea Party, and conservative think institutes. These organizations are responsible for organizing rallies, mobilizing supporters, and participating in advocacy efforts on both a local and national level (Mayhew, 2011).

2. Media Influence

There is a significant presence of conservatives in many media channels, including talk radio, conservative television networks, and internet platforms. According to Stroud (2017), prominent figures in the conservative media, such as Rush Limbaugh and Sean Hannity, have emerged as powerful voices.

3. Legal Challenges

Frequently, conservative organizations may resort to the legal system to dispute laws and regulations that they consider to be in violation of the Constitution or to be in opposition to their ideals. In this context, litigation on matters such as religious liberty and liberties guaranteed by the Second Amendment is included.

4. Electoral Engagement

At every level of government, conservatives are involved in political politics and actively engage in the process. They contribute to the campaigns of politicians who share their conservative ideals and principles, and they try to ensure that these individuals are elected (Mayhew, 2011). They also express their support and endorsement of such candidates.

5. Grassroots Education

The education and outreach efforts of conservative groups are given a significant amount of importance. They provide resources, hold seminars, and generate publications to educate their followers and the wider public on conservative values and policies.

Intellectual Leaders and Think Tanks

There is a multitude of intellectual leaders and think tanks that provide intellectual underpinnings for the conservative movement's objectives, which is beneficial to the cause by providing intellectual support. Thomas Sowell and Milton Friedman are two prominent conservative thinkers who have made significant contributions to economically and socially conservative philosophy (Sowell, 1980). Both of these individuals have offered ideas that have influence. Think tanks that adhere to conservative ideology, such as The Heritage Foundation, are responsible for doing research and putting up policy suggestions that shape conservative activism and policymaking.

The Impact on American Society

Several facets of American society have been significantly altered as a result of the conservative counterattack, including the following:

1. Policy Battles

There has been success for conservatives in their efforts to press for policy changes that are in line with their agenda. The reduction of taxes, the loosening of regulations, and the appointment of conservative justices to federal courts are all included in this. According to Mayhew (2011), the country has moved in a path that is more following conservative values as a result of these policy debates.

2. Political Polarization

The ideological conflict that exists between conservatives and progressives is one factor that has led to the polarization of political opinion in the United States. There has been a growing difficulty in locating areas of agreement and developing solutions that are acceptable to both parties (Abramowitz & Saunders, 2008). This is because both sides are becoming more passionate about their viewpoints.

3. Media Landscape

The proliferation of conservative talk radio and the preponderance of conservative television networks are two examples of how conservatives have disrupted the traditional media landscape. These venues contribute to the propagation of conservative ideas and opinions by providing a forum for conservative voices and contributing to the dissemination of conservative ideas (Stroud, 2017).

4. Cultural Debates

Throughout cultural discussions about topics such as abortion, LGBTQ+ rights, and religious liberty, conservatives have been at the forefront of the conversation. These arguments are a reflection of the effect that conservative ideals and beliefs have had on the society of the United States.

5. Civic Engagement

Conservative grassroots organizations have been successful in encouraging their members to participate in civic activities. According to Mayhew (2011), conservative activists frequently participate in local community initiatives, political campaigns, and lobbying activities. Others may also be active.

Conclusion

For the past several years, one of the most distinguishing characteristics of American politics has been the conservative defense against the progressive agenda. As both sides continue to vehemently fight for their distinct conceptions of the United States of America, the conflict of ideas continues to have an impact on the nation's policies, elections, and cultural affairs.

We will investigate more aspects of this ideological conflict in the chapters that are to come. These aspects will include the role that culture plays, the influence that it has on the economy, and the potential ways forward for a society that is struggling with significant ideological divisions.

References:

Abramowitz, A. I., & Saunders, K. L. (2008). Is Polarization a Myth? The Journal of Politics, 70(2), 542-555.

Friedman, M. (1962). Capitalism and Freedom. University of Chicago Press.

Mayhew, D. R. (2011). Electoral Realignments: A Critique of an American Genre. Yale University Press.

Sowell, T. (1980). Knowledge and Decisions. Basic Books.

Stroud, N. J. (2017). Polarization and Partisan Selective Exposure. Journal of Communication, 67(4), 515-535.

Part 3: The Role of Free Markets

In the continuous ideological conflict that is taking place within the United States, the idea of free markets has a fundamental position in the thought and policy of conservatives. There are others who believe that free markets are beneficial because they encourage innovation, economic prosperity, and individual liberty. The concepts, practices, and ramifications of this fundamental tenet of conservative ideology are investigated in this chapter, which dives into the role that free markets play in the conservative assault against the progressive agenda.

Introduction

Since the beginning of conservative philosophy, the concept of free markets has been considered a fundamental value. This view is based on the idea that individuals, and not governments, should be the ones to decide what kinds of commodities and services are created, how they are dispersed, and at what rates they are sold. One of the most contentious issues in the ideological conflict between conservatives and progressives is the question of what role free markets should play in the economy.

The argument put up by conservatives is that free markets not only result in economic development but also act as a safeguard for the privileges and rights of individuals. Conservatives argue that people are best able to pursue their interests and enjoy their liberties when restrictions on government interference are placed and market forces are allowed to function. This chapter examines the conceptual foundations of free-market conservatism, as well as its ramifications for public policy and the current discussion that surrounds the positive aspects of this ideology.

Intellectual Foundations

The roots of free-market conservatism may be traced back to classical liberal intellectuals and economists who advocated for the ideas of economic independence and minimal government intrusion. These individuals laid the intellectual groundwork for free-market conservatism. This philosophy has been developed with the contributions of some important personalities, including:

1. Adam Smith

Adam Smith was a Scottish economist who is often considered to be the "father" of modern economics. He was also a significant player in the creation of the concept of free market economic ideas. Smith contended in his landmark work "An Inquiry into the Nature and Causes of the Wealth of Nations" (1776) that people pursuing their self-interest within a framework of voluntary commerce would unwittingly enhance the well-being of society as a whole. Smith's study was published in 1776. He was the one who first proposed the idea of the "invisible hand," which suggested that markets might self-regulate and effectively distribute resources (Smith, 1776).

2. Friedrich Hayek

In the 20th century, the Austrian economist Friedrich Hayek developed and enlarged upon the principles that Adam Smith had proposed. Hayek stated in his article "The Use of Knowledge in Society" (1945) that centralized planning and government control were bound to fail because they could never hold the distributed information held by countless individuals in a market system. He concluded that this was the single most important factor in the failure of these two systems. According to Hayek (1945), he placed a strong emphasis on the function that markets play in organizing this geographically scattered information and enabling effective resource allocation.

3. Milton Friedman

In addition to being a famous proponent of free-market economics, the American economist Milton Friedman made substantial contributions to the intellectual underpinnings of conservatism. His book "Capitalism and Freedom" was published in 1962, and it stated that economic freedom was necessary for political freedom as well as individual liberty. Friedman advocated for the abolition of occupational licensure, school choice, and floating exchange rates as a method to increase economic and personal freedom (Friedman, 1962). He also advocated for the elimination of school choice.

4. The Austrian School

A significant contribution to the development of free-market conservatism was made by the Austrian School of Economics, which included the contributions of intellectuals such as Ludwig von Mises and Carl Menger. Both Menger (1871) and Mises (1949) were prominent economists who placed a strong emphasis on the significance of human choice, entrepreneurialism, and the subjective character of value in the context of economic transactions.

Policy Implications

The concepts of free-market conservatism have a significant influence on a wide variety of subjects that fall under the purview of policy. Conservatives claim that less government engagement in the economy leads to better economic efficiency, innovation, and individual opportunity. The following are some of the most important policy consequences that free-market conservatism has:

1. Deregulation

Conservatives are in favor of decreasing the number of rules imposed by the government, which they consider to be onerous and detrimental to economic expansion. They claim that excessive regulation may be detrimental to the generation of jobs and can also stifle entrepreneurial endeavors. Under the Trump administration, deregulation was a significant policy effort, with various regulations taken back (Office of Information and Regulatory Affairs, n.d.).

2. Tax Cuts

Reducing taxes is a defining characteristic of conservative economic policy. One strategy that is considered to be effective in boosting economic growth, encouraging job creation, and stimulating investment is to reduce taxes, particularly those that are imposed on individuals and corporations. According to the Internal Revenue

Service (n.d.), the Tax Cuts and Jobs Act of 2017 was a notable victory for conservative policymakers since it achieved the reduction of tax rates for both corporations and individuals.

3. Limited Government Spending

On the other hand, conservatives stress the significance of limiting the expenditure of the government to avoid budget deficits and debt that cannot be sustained. According to their argument, a smaller government is less likely to interfere with the operations of the market and the decisions that individuals make. According to the Congressional Budget Office (2021), one of the primary policy goals of free-market conservatives is to work toward achieving budgetary prudence.

4. Free Trade

Conservatives who advocate for free trade policies and advocate for the elimination of trade obstacles and tariffs are known as free-market conservatives. They claim that free trade increases the number of economic options available, reduces the costs that consumers pay, and encourages global collaboration. According to the Office of the United States Trade Representative (n.d.), conservatives have shown their support for trade deals such as the United States-Mexico-Canada Agreement (USMCA).

5. Monetary Policy

It is common for conservatives to advocate for a monetary policy that is consistent, predictable, and that restricts the government's involvement in the financial markets and the currency market. They argue for the independence of central banks, such as the Federal Reserve, to prevent inflationary pressures from occurring (Federal Reserve System, n.d.).

The Debate Surrounding Free Markets

Although free markets are a fundamental tenet of conservative ideology, they are not without their share of dispute and contention. Some people believe that unrestrained markets might result in unequal distribution of income, potential for exploitation, and instability in the economy. They argue that to redress social inequities and repair market failures, the intervention of the government is required. The disagreements that have arisen about the function of the government in the economy continue to be a primary source of friction in the political arena of the United States.

Conclusion

It is impossible to exaggerate the significance of free markets in connection with conservative philosophy and policy. For conservatives, the ideas of economic freedom, minimal government intrusion, and individual opportunity are crucial to their vision for America. While some who support free markets say that they are beneficial to economic progress and individual liberty, those who oppose them claim that they may make inequality worse and necessitate the existence of government control.

As the ideological conflict between conservatives and progressives continues to unfold, the subsequent chapters will investigate additional aspects of this ideological conflict. These aspects will include the impact on culture, the influence on society, and the potential ways forward for a nation that is struggling with profound ideological differences.

References:

Congressional Budget Office. (2021). The Budget and Economic Outlook: 2021 to 2031. https://www.cbo.gov/publication/56965

Federal Reserve System. (n.d.). About the Fed. https://www.federalreserve.gov/aboutthefed/

Friedman, M. (1962). Capitalism and Freedom. University of Chicago Press.

Hayek, F. A. (1945). The Use of Knowledge in Society. The American Economic Review, 35(4), 519-530.

Internal Revenue Service. (n.d.). Tax Cuts and Jobs Act. https://www.irs.gov/newsroom/tax-cuts-and-jobs-act

Menger, C. (1871). Principles of Economics. Ludwig von Mises Institute.

Mises, L. (1949). Human Action: A Treatise on Economics. Yale University Press.

Office of Information and Regulatory Affairs. (n.d.). About. https://www.reginfo.gov/public/jsp/Utilities/about.jsp

Office of the United States Trade Representative. (n.d.). United States-Mexico-Canada Agreement (USMCA). https://ustr.gov/trade-agreements/free-trade-agreements/united-states-mexico-canada-agreement

Smith, A. (1776). An Inquiry into the Nature and Causes of the Wealth of Nations. London: W. Strahan and T. Cadell.

Part 4: The Importance of Individual Rights

One of the most important concepts in conservative philosophy and politics is the idea of individual rights, which is at the center of the continuous ideological conflict that is taking place within the United States. The safeguarding of individual rights, especially those that are written in the Constitution, is, according to conservatives, of the utmost importance to maintain liberty and restrict the extent to which the government may get involved. Within the context of the conservative assault against the progressive agenda, this chapter dives into the significance of individual rights. It investigates the concepts, policies, and ramifications of this basic part of conservative ideology.

Introduction

The concept of individual rights is fundamental to the American experience. It is entrenched in the Declaration of Independence, which states that all persons are endowed with certain rights that cannot be taken away from them. These rights include the right to life, liberty, and the pursuit of happiness. Further codification of these rights may be found in the Constitution of the United States of America and the Bill of Rights, which together form a foundation for limited government and the preservation of individual liberties.

The argument put out by conservatives is that individual rights act as a defense mechanism against the overreach and tyranny of the government. They argue that a government that recognizes and maintains these rights helps to cultivate a society in which individuals are free to pursue their objectives, make their own decisions, and live their lives without undue interference from the government. A discussion of the conceptual foundations of individual rights, the consequences of those rights for public policy, and the current controversy that surrounds the interpretation and implementation of such rights is presented in this chapter.

Intellectual Foundations

In conservative philosophy, the philosophical roots of the value of individual rights are firmly anchored in the ideas of classical liberalism and the writings of famous intellectuals who championed these goals. These concepts and writings are the basis of conservative nationalism. Among the most influential persons in the development of this facet of conservatism are the following:

1. John Locke

The ideas that the English philosopher John Locke expressed on natural rights and the social compact had a significant influence on the Founding Fathers of the United States of America. Locke contended that people have natural rights to their own lives, their liberty, and their property and that governments are established to safeguard these rights. According to Locke (1689), his theories were crucial in laying the foundation for the American philosophy of individual rights.

2. Thomas Jefferson

One of the key architects of the Declaration of Independence, Thomas Jefferson, is credited with making the famous declaration that individuals are entitled to certain rights that cannot be taken away from them. These rights include the right to life, liberty, and the pursuit of happiness. According to the Declaration of Independence from 1776, Jefferson's thoughts contributed to the formation of the fundamental concepts that underpin American democracy.

3. James Madison

In the process of establishing the Bill of Rights, James Madison, who is sometimes referred to as the "Father of the Constitution," was an extremely important contributor. The incorporation of essential clauses that preserve freedoms of speech, religion, and the right to carry weapons was made possible as a result of his dedication to the protection of individual liberties through constitutional changes (The Bill of Rights, 1791).

4. The philosopher Friedrich Hayek

Even though he is most recognized for his contributions to the field of economics, the Austrian economist Friedrich Hayek also placed a strong emphasis on the significance of individual rights. It was in his work "The Constitution of Liberty" (1960) that Hayek claimed that a free society is dependent on the rule of law to safeguard individual rights and avoid arbitrary actions taken by the government (Hayek, 1960).

Policy Implications

A substantial number of policy issues are associated with the significance of individual rights for conservatives. Advocates for policies and legal frameworks that give the protection of individual liberties the highest priority are these individuals. The following are some of the most important policy sectors that are impacted by this conservative principle:

1. Freedom of Speech

The right to freedom of expression is a basic principle that is strongly defended by conservatives. They claim that people should be allowed to freely express their thoughts and views without the fear of being censored or punished by the government. Conservatives have shown their support for legal conflicts over free speech, notably those that take place on college campuses and on social media platforms (First Amendment, 1791).

2. Second Amendment Rights

On the other hand, conservatives support the protection of the right to carry weapons that is provided by the Second Amendment. They contend that the right to possess and carry weapons is necessary for self-protection and as a defensive mechanism against the oppression of the government. A significant number of conservatives have shown their support for legal challenges to gun restriction legislation (Second Amendment, 1791).

3. Religious Freedom

Conservatives believe that the right to freedom of religion is an essential component of individual rights. They contend that people and religious groups should not be forced to violate their strongly held values by government demands. They claim that this should not be the case. Conservatives have been the most vocal advocates for cases that include religious freedom, such as the one involving Hobby Lobby (Burwell v. Hobby Lobby, 2014).

4. Property Rights

Conservatives place a strong emphasis on the protection of property rights because they believe that these rights are fundamental to the freedom of the person and the economy. (Fifth Amendment, 1791) They are opposed to the government taking private property without providing reasonable compensation and they are in favor of placing restrictions on eminent domain legislation.

5. Confidentiality

On the other hand, conservatives argue that people have a right to privacy, which includes the right to be protected from undue government monitoring and intervention in personal concerns. Legal matters that pertain to privacy, such as the implementation of the Fourth Amendment in the digital era, give rise to substantial concerns among conservatives (Fourth Amendment, 1791).

The Debate Surrounding Individual Rights

Even though the significance of individual rights is a fundamental tenet of conservative ideology, there is still ongoing dispute on the extent to which these rights may be exercised and the boundaries that they can be pushed to. Certain rights, such as the right to carry weapons or the right to religious freedom, are said to be in potential conflict with the rights and well-being of other people, according to the arguments of certain individuals. The question of how to strike a balance between individual rights and collective benefit is still being debated and interpreted by the legal system.

Conclusion

One of the most essential pillars of conservative thought and policy is the safeguarding of individual rights. Conservatives argue that these rights, which are incorporated in the Constitution and are founded on the ideals of liberty, serve as a protection against the expansion of the government and the degradation of personal liberties. Even if the ideological conflict between conservatives and progressives continues to have a significant impact on the political landscape in the United States, the concepts of individual rights continue to be at the core of the conservative vision for the country.

As the chapters that follow explore additional dimensions of this ideological conflict, including the impact on culture, the importance of individual rights will continue to play a vital part in the ongoing battle for the future of the United States of America. This is due to the effect that individual rights have on society as well as the potential ways ahead for a nation that is divided by significant ideological divides.

References:

Declaration of Independence. (1776). National Archives. https://www.archives.gov/founding-docs/declaration

The Bill of Rights. (1791). National Archives. https://www.archives.gov/founding-docs/bill-of-rights
Burwell v. Hobby Lobby, 573 U.S. 682 (2014).

Fifth Amendment to the United States Constitution. (1791). Legal Information Institute. https://www.law.cornell.edu/constitution/fifth_amendment

First Amendment to the United States Constitution. (1791). Legal Information Institute. https://www.law.cornell.edu/constitution/first_amendment

Fourth Amendment to the United States Constitution. (1791). Legal Information Institute. https://www.law.cornell.edu/constitution/fourth_amendment

Hayek, F. (1960). The Constitution of Liberty. University of Chicago Press.

Part 5: The Impact of Culture

Introduction

The United States of America has a culture that acts as a mirror of the beliefs, traditions, and values of its people. This culture has a dynamic influence on the norms that emerge in society. The continuous ideological confrontation between conservative and progressive values is a prominent subject in the nation's political and social debate. Both sides propose different views for the future of the country, and the way in which culture plays a role in forming and being molded by these visions is a central topic of discussion. In this chapter, we look into the vital role that culture plays in the battleground of ideologies. We investigate traditional values, significant topics in the culture war, and the influence that media and entertainment have on molding public opinion.

The Role of Traditional Values

Those who adhere to the conservative ideology believe that traditional family structures are essential for maintaining social order. They emphasize heterosexual marriage and traditional gender roles. According to the Pew Research Center's 2020 report, conservative values are founded on the core concept that the nuclear family is essential to the overall well-being of society. With many people gaining moral direction from their faith and pushing for religious freedom in public life and policy discussions, religion also plays a substantial role in conservative ideology (Pew Research Center, 2019). This implies that religion plays a large role in conservative ideology. Additionally, according to the Pew Research Center (2019), the conservative philosophy places a significant focus on the importance of individual responsibility and self-sufficiency above reliance on the help provided by the government.

The Culture War

Many controversial subjects are included in the culture war, including immigration, education, LGBTQ+ rights, and abortion. On the issue of abortion, conservatives traditionally take a pro-life stance, whereas progressives place a higher priority on reproductive rights and women's autonomy (Pew Research Center, 2020). According to the Pew Research Center's 2020 report, the battle over LGBTQ+ rights highlights the contradiction between traditionalism and inclusion, while immigration policies reflect different perspectives on the values that comprise American society. Education has emerged as a central topic, with disagreements over the curriculum mirroring wider ideological splits. Additionally, the question of transgender rights has prompted a huge discussion on conventional gender standards and inclusion (The New York Times, 2021).

The Role of Media and Entertainment

According to the Pew Research Center's 2020 report, conservatives frequently criticize mainstream media for what they perceive to be a liberal slant, which has led to the proliferation of conservative media sites as alternatives. As a result of conservatives' criticism of the entertainment industry, notably Hollywood, for supporting progressive principles, there have been requests for more entertainment that is in line with conservative ideas (The Hollywood Reporter, 2020).

The Conservative Response

According to surveys conducted by the Pew Research Center in 2020, conservative media sites have become increasingly prominent as alternate sources of information and perspectives. Grassroots groups such as the Tea Party and the Million Americans for America (MAGA) movement are examples of conservative mobilization around cultural and political problems. Conservatives, on the other hand, argue for reforms in educational material that match traditional values (National Review, 2021).

Final Thoughts

In the United States, culture continues to be a crucial battlefield between conservatives and progressives, since it shapes public discourse and influences the values that are held by all members of society. At the same time as the country is struggling to overcome these ideological differences, the future course of its cultural landscape is dependent on the outcome of this struggle. The discussion that is still going on is a reflection of the variety that exists within American society as well as the continual battle to define the identity and values of the nation in a world that is always shifting.

The culture of the United States is a dynamic and important force that defines and reflects the values, beliefs, and goals of many groups within the continuous ideological conflict that is taking place inside the

United States to this day. Within the context of the conservative counterattack against the progressive agenda, this chapter digs into the myriad ways in which culture acts as an influence. It investigates the ways in which culture functions as both a battlefield and a foundation in the ideological fight. It encompasses conventional values, religious beliefs, family relationships, and controversial themes such as transgenderism.

Part 5: The Impact of Culture (Continued)

The political environment in the United States places a significant amount of importance on culture, which can be defined as the collective expression of a society's beliefs and traditions. Conservatives contend that culture is not just a mirror that reflects their values, but also a strong force that influences conduct sets standards, and contributes to the moral fabric of the nation. They say this because culture is a reflection of their principles. The continuous ideological confrontation between conservatives and progressives is the topic of discussion in this chapter, in which we investigate how culture impacts and responds to the conflict.

The Role of Traditional Values

Values that have been passed down through generations are the foundation of conservative philosophy and society. These values include a dedication to the family, faith, personal responsibility, and a restriction on the role that the government plays in the lives of individuals. These principles, according to conservatives, are necessary for the stability and moral fortitude of society, and they contend that they are crucial.

Family Values

When it comes to conservative culture, traditional family values are at the most important. When it comes to the establishment of a stable society, conservatives place a high priority on the nuclear family unit. They emphasize the significance of heterosexual marriages, conventional gender roles, and the role that the nuclear family plays in providing stability, support, and moral direction (Pew Research Center, 2020).

Religious Faith

In conservative society, religion is considered to be of utmost importance. A significant number of conservatives are strongly religious, and their moral and ethical convictions are frequently influenced by their faith. According to the Pew Research Center (2019), they argue for the protection of religious freedom and say that individuals and institutions should be able to follow their faith without interference from the government.

Individual Responsibility

The concept of individual responsibility is given a significant amount of weight in conservative society. Individuals should accept personal responsibility for their activities and well-being, according to conservatives, rather than relying on government support or entitlement programs. Conservatives claim that this strategy is more effective. According to Pew Research Center (2019), one of the distinguishing characteristics of conservative culture is the belief in the importance of self-reliance and individual accountability.

The Culture War

The term "culture war" is an effective way to express the continuing ideological dispute that exists between conservatives and progressives about matters of culture. This lengthy conflict covers controversial arguments concerning a variety of themes, including but not limited to abortion, LGBTQ+ rights, gender identity, immigration regulation, and educational policies. Not only do these challenges reflect cultural inflection points, but they also symbolize a more general conflict of ideals.

Abortion

Within the context of the culture war, abortion continues to be one of the most divisive topics. Pro-life policies are often supported by conservatives, who maintain that the beginning of life occurs at the time of conception. The progressives advocate for reproductive rights and the ability of women to make their own decisions, while the conservatives strive to restrict or remove access to abortion to emphasize the sanctity of life (Pew Research Center, 2020).

LGBTQ+ Rights

The LGBTQ+ rights movement has sparked strong disputes over traditional cultural norms, such as marriage between people of the same gender and rights for transgender people. There is frequently a difference of opinion between progressive ideas of equality and inclusion and traditional conservative principles. According to the Pew Research Center's publication from 2020, these discussions highlight the contradiction that exists between cultural conservatism and social liberalism.

Immigration

Another cultural flashpoint that has arisen as a result of the ideological clash is immigration. The conservative movement advocates for more stringent immigration laws and border controls, believing that the protection of American culture and values necessitates the establishment of secure borders. Progressives, on the other hand, frequently push for immigration policies that are more humane and inclusive (Pew Research Center, 2020).

Education

A battleground in the culture war has emerged in the realm of education, with conservatives expressing their worries on the impact of progressive ideology in educational institutions such as schools and universities. Progressives advocate for inclusiveness, diversity, and the absorption of a wider range of viewpoints in education, but conventional curriculum and values in education are something that they want to preserve (Pew Research Center, 2020).

Transgenderism

The battle over transgenderism has emerged as a significant cultural flashpoint in recent years. Concerns have been voiced by conservatives over rules that pertain to transgender persons, notably in areas such as access to restrooms and sports. They contend that these measures provide a challenge to the conventional gender standards and may have outcomes that were not intended. Progressives, on the other hand, are advocates for transgender rights and inclusiveness, and they place a strong emphasis on the significance of recognizing gender identity (The New York Times, 2021).

The Role of Media and Entertainment

The media and entertainment industries are significant cultural influences that contribute to the continuous ideological war in the world. There have been several occasions when conservatives have voiced their worry about what they see to be a liberal bias in mainstream media and entertainment. They contend that this implicit prejudice might result in a one-sided depiction of topics as well as a lack of variety in the opinions that are presented.

Mainstream Media

Conservatives regularly criticize mainstream media outlets, arguing that these channels give more weight to liberal opinions and can be dismissive of conservative points of view. The growth of conservative media sources as alternatives to what many conservatives see to be a biased establishment has been a direct result of the perception of bias that exists in the media (Pew Research Center, 2020).

Entertainment Industry

Additionally, the entertainment sector, which encompasses Hollywood as well as the music industry, has been a subject of controversy. Conservatives argue that these sectors not only promote progressive principles but also frequently contradict the cultural norms that have been established over time. According to The Hollywood Reporter (2020), this has resulted in requests for entertainment options that are more supportive of conservative policies.

The Conservative Response

The conservative movement has tried several different tactics to promote its ideals and exert influence over cultural narratives in response to what they see to be cultural challenges and developments.

Conservative Media

As alternate sources of news and opinion, conservative media channels such as Fox News, talk radio, and internet platforms have been increasingly prominent in recent years. According to the Pew Research Center's 2020 report, these sources offer a forum for conservative views and perspectives, therefore addressing what many conservatives see to be bias in the media industry.

Grassroots Activism

There have been conservative grassroots groups that have galvanized people over cultural and political problems. Some examples of these movements are the Tea Party movement and the Make America Great Again (MAGA) movement. According to The Heritage Foundation's research from 2020, these movements emphasize conservative ideals and strive to exert influence on policy and cultural disputes.

Education and Curriculum

Conservatives have also grown more active in campaigning for reforms in education, notably in the curriculum of elementary and secondary schools as well as those of colleges and universities. A method that is more conservative-friendly and more balanced in its approach to teaching history, civics, and social concerns is something that they want to encourage (National Review, 2021).

Conclusion

In the continuous ideological fight between conservatives and progressives, culture is a factor that is both dynamic and important throughout the conflict. Traditional values, religious beliefs, the dynamics of families, and controversial topics like transgenderism are all factors that contribute to the fabric of cultural disputes that is so rich and diverse. The conflict that is known as the culture war comprises not just disagreements about particular legislation, but also a more general conflict regarding the principles that constitute American society.

As significant cultural influences, the media and entertainment industries have also come under examination. Conservatives have expressed concerns about what they perceive to be prejudice and a lack of representation of their ideas in these areas. For their part, conservatives have responded by establishing their own media channels, participating in grassroots activity, and advocating for changes in the educational system.

The influence of culture will continue to play a pivotal role in shaping the future of the United States of America as the chapters that follow explore additional dimensions of this ideological conflict. These dimensions include the influence on society, the significance of individual rights, and the potential paths forward for a nation that is divided by profound ideological differences.

References:

Pew Research Center. (2019). The Global God Divide. https://www.pewresearch.org/global/2019/04/22/appendix-a-the-global-god-divide/

Pew Research Center. (2020). What Unites and Divides Urban, Suburban and Rural Communities. https://www.pewresearch.org/social-trends/2020/05/22/partisan-divides-on-political-values-widen-especially-over-racial-justice-and-immigration/

The Heritage Foundation. (2020). The Tea Party Movement: A Bibliographic Essay. https://www.heritage.org/tea-party/report/the-tea-party-movement-bibliographic-essay

The Hollywood Reporter. (2020). Hollywood's 50 Most Powerful TV Czars of 2020. https://www.hollywoodreporter.com/lists/hollywoods-50-powerful-tv-czars-2020-1308009

The National Review. (2021). How Conservatives Can Take Back the Education Issue. https://www.nationalreview.com/2021/02/how-conservatives-can-take-back-the-education-issue/

The New York Times. (2021). The Fight Over Trans Rights Is a Battle for America's Soul. https://www.nytimes.com/2021/06/25/opinion/lgbtq-trans-rights-conservatives.html

Part 6: The Impact on Society

The ideological clash between conservatives and progressives in the United States has had far-reaching consequences that extend beyond the realm of politics. It has left an indelible mark on American society, influencing various aspects of daily life, values, and cultural norms. This chapter delves into the multifaceted impact of this ideological battle on society, including its effects on political dynamics, the rise of polarization, cultural shifts, and the role of activism and social movements.

Introduction

The ideological struggle between conservatives and progressives has been a defining feature of American society in recent years. While it is often most visible in the political arena, its influence goes well beyond elections and policy debates. This chapter explores how the clash of ideas has shaped and transformed American society, impacting the way people interact, the values they hold, and the cultural shifts that have emerged as a result.

The Influence on American Politics

The battle between conservatives and progressives has significantly shaped the landscape of American politics, influencing elections, policy decisions, and the broader political discourse.

Elections and political behavior

The ideological divide in American society has translated into distinct voting patterns and political behavior. Voters increasingly identify with political parties that align with their values and beliefs, contributing to political polarization. Elections often hinge on issues such as healthcare, climate change, immigration, and social justice, with candidates representing contrasting ideological positions (Pew Research Center, 2020).

Policy Debates and Legislative Stalemates

The ideological battle has permeated policy debates, leading to legislative gridlock on key issues. Conservatives and progressives vigorously contest policies related to healthcare, taxation, immigration, environmental regulations, and more. This ideological impasse has at times hindered the ability to pass comprehensive reforms and find common ground (Brookings Institution, 2019).

The Rise of Polarization

One of the most evident consequences of the ideological struggle is the increasing polarization of American society. This polarization extends beyond politics and has implications for social interactions, media consumption, and the overall functioning of the nation.

Social Divisions

Political polarization has infiltrated social relationships, straining interactions among family members, friends, and colleagues who hold opposing political views. Political identity has become a central aspect of personal identity, leading to the fragmentation of social networks and reducing the willingness to engage in constructive dialogue (Pew Research Center, 2020).

Media Echo Chambers

Polarization has reshaped the media landscape, with conservatives and progressives consuming news from sources that align with their ideological stances. This phenomenon has given rise to echo chambers, where individuals are exposed to information and viewpoints that reinforce their existing beliefs. Media outlets catering to specific ideological orientations have contributed to this trend (Pew Research Center, 2018).

Cultural Shifts and Identity Politics

The ideological battle has sparked significant cultural shifts, shaping societal norms, values, and the way issues related to identity are perceived and addressed.

LGBTQ+ Rights

The fight for LGBTQ+ rights has resulted in profound cultural changes. The legalization of same-sex marriage, debates over transgender rights, and increasing acceptance of LGBTQ+ individuals represent some of the shifts in societal attitudes and policies. However, these changes have also been met with resistance from conservatives, leading to clashes over the pace and extent of LGBTQ+ rights (Pew Research Center, 2020).

Racial Justice

Issues related to racial justice, including protests against police violence, calls for criminal justice reform, and debates over the removal of Confederate monuments, have roiled American society. The battle over racial justice has prompted discussions about systemic racism, historical legacies, and the role of race in shaping American institutions (Pew Research Center, 2020).

Gender Equality

The quest for gender equality has been a focal point of cultural shifts, with debates over gender pay gaps, reproductive rights, and gender identity challenging traditional norms and roles. These discussions have highlighted tensions between the protection of individual rights and the preservation of traditional values (Pew Research Center, 2020).

Immigration

Immigration has been a contentious issue at the intersection of cultural and political debates. Conservatives emphasize border security and the preservation of American culture, while progressives advocate for a more inclusive and compassionate approach to immigration policy. These differing perspectives reflect deeper ideological divisions (Pew Research Center, 2020).

The Role of Activism and Social Movements

The ideological struggle has catalyzed activism and social movements on both sides of the divide, leading to shifts in public opinion, policy changes, and social transformation.

Grassroots Movements

Conservative grassroots movements, such as the Tea Party and the Make America Great Again (MAGA) movement, have mobilized supporters to advocate for conservative values and policies. They have played a pivotal role in elections, policy debates, and the overall direction of the conservative movement (The Heritage Foundation, 2020).

Progressive Activism

Progressive activists have also been instrumental in pushing for change. Movements like Black Lives Matter, the Women's March, and climate activism have drawn attention to critical issues and influenced policy discussions. These movements prioritize social justice, equality, and progressive policy reforms (The Washington Post, 2020).

The ideological conflict that exists between conservatives and progressives in the United States is a phenomena that is deeply ingrained and goes beyond simple political disagreement. It permeates every aspect of American life and is transforming the terrain of society. This collision of ideas, which is defined by a significant divergence in values and visions for the future, has important consequences not only for the political arena but also for the social fabric, cultural norms, and the collective consciousness of the nation. Specifically, this clash of ideas has enormous implications for the political arena. The purpose of this chapter is to go deeper into the societal repercussions of this ideological debate. We will examine its impact on the political dynamics, the increase of polarization, cultural transformations, and the growing role that activism and social movements play in bringing about change.

The Political Arena: A Battlefield of Ideas

There is little doubt that the ideological gap has brought about a transformation in American politics, ushering in a new age in which elections and the policy-making process have become battlegrounds for competing visions of the United States of America. In the polarization of electoral choices, where voters are increasingly linked along ideological lines, topics such as healthcare reform, climate change policies, and immigration laws have become crucial to political campaigns. This division is obvious in the fact that voters are increasingly united along different ideological lines. Such polarization has resulted in legislative stalemates, as seen by the many impasses that occur in Congress. These impasses are caused by political stances, which frequently end in a gridlock, which makes it difficult to enact substantial legislation.

Societal Polarization: Beyond Political Divides

The influence of this ideological conflict goes far into the realm of social life, where polarization has contributed to the formation of divides that affect the dynamics of individual relationships and interactions within communities. This phenomenon is not confined to the realm of political speech; rather, it has an impact on social relationships and frequently results in a sense of alienation amongst those who have contrasting political perspectives. This separation has been further exacerbated by the emergence of media that is ideologically driven, which has resulted in the creation of echo chambers that serve to affirm preexisting ideas and contribute to the homogeneity of attitudes within in-groups, while simultaneously alienating those who hold opposing viewpoints.

Cultural Transformations and Identity Politics

Significant cultural developments have also been brought about as a result of the ideological conflict, notably in areas that are related to identity politics, such as the rights of LGBTQ+ individuals, racial justice, and gender equality advocates. Each of these spheres has been the site of important societal debates and legislative reforms, which are reflective of a larger conflict over the path that society should take to advance and the acknowledgment of different identities. As an illustration, the expansion of LGBTQ+ rights, which includes the legalization of marriage between people of the same gender, has represented a substantial shift in the norms of society, although it is met with hostility by conservative elements. In a similar vein, the movement for racial justice and gender equality continues to question the institutions that are now in place, bringing to light the constant conflict that exists between cultural values and society standards.

The Ascendancy of Activism and Social Movements

As a result of movements on both ends of the ideological spectrum coming together to fight for their respective causes, activism has developed as a significant factor in the process of molding public discourse and policy. The political debate has been significantly steered by conservative movements like the Tea Party, which have also had a considerable impact on the outcomes of policy discussions. Conversely, progressive groups, such as Black Lives Matter and climate activism, have pushed vital concerns to the forefront, questioning conventional conventions and pressing for substantial reforms. These movements are a reflection of the dynamic nature of American culture, which is characterized by activity that acts as a catalyst for change and pushes the boundaries of what is politically and socially possible.

Conclusion: An Ongoing Ideological Confrontation

A distinguishing characteristic of modern American culture is the ideological conflict that exists between conservatives and progressives. This conflict has far-reaching repercussions that go well beyond the bounds of political discourse. The landscape of society has been transformed as a result of this conflict, which has had an impact on cultural norms and values as well as the collective quest of justice and equality. As this ideological conflict continues to play out, it will surely have a significant impact on the future course of the United States. This highlights the significance of conversation, understanding, and compromise to successfully navigate the complexity of this continuing fight.

The ramifications of this ideological conflict are quite significant since they touch upon the core of the American identity as well as the path that the nation would hopefully take in the future. Because the United States of America is struggling to overcome these obstacles, it is becoming increasingly evident that there is a need for a fresh commitment to the ideals of democracy, inclusion, and mutual respect. This would provide a road toward reconciliation and togetherness in a society that is severely divided.

References:

Brookings Institution. (2019). Polarization and Policy: The Impact of Political Polarization in the U.S. Congress. https://www.brookings.edu/research/polarization-and-policy-the-impact-of-political-polarization-in-the-u-s-congress/

Pew Research Center. (2018). Political Polarization in the American Public. https://www.pewresearch.org/politics/2014/06/12/political-polarization-in-the-american-public/

Pew Research Center. (2020). What Unites and Divides Urban, Suburban and Rural Communities. https://www.pewresearch.org/social-trends/2020/05/22/partisan-divides-on-political-values-widen-especially-over-racial-justice-and-immigration/

The Heritage Foundation. (2020). The Tea Party Movement: A Bibliographic Essay. https://www.heritage.org/tea-party/report/the-tea-party-movement-bibliographic-essay

The Washington Post. (2020). How the Black Lives Matter Movement Went Mainstream. https://www.washingtonpost.com/graphics/2020/lifestyle/how-black-lives-matter-shifted-american-politics/

Part 7: Conclusion

Throughout the preceding portions of this chapter, we have thoroughly investigated the severe ideological conflict that has been taking place within the society of the United States. The conflict between conservative and progressive principles has had significant repercussions for the nation, including an impact on politics, polarization, cultural developments, and the function of activism. In this last section, we will present a detailed overview of the chapter as well as insights into the overall influence that this continuous conflict has had on the United States of America.

The Clash of Ideas

These profoundly ingrained contrasts in values, beliefs, and policy goals have been the defining characteristics of the ideological conflict that has been going on in the United States between conservatives and progressives. The scope of this conflict, which has been a defining characteristic of modern politics, goes beyond simple disagreements in ideology and political rhetoric. It exemplifies a fundamental disagreement between opposing viewpoints about the function of the government, the rights of individuals, and the objectives for the future of the nation.

The most obvious manifestation of this collision of ideas can be seen in the political arena, where elections have become battlegrounds for rival visions of the United States of America. A harsh division of the electorate has resulted from the fact that voters are increasingly aligning themselves with political parties that mirror their ideals.

Arguments over public policy concerning topics such as healthcare, climate change, immigration, and social justice have become indicative of the ideological gap that exists in the United States.

The Rise of Polarization

The conflict over ideology has resulted in the formation of a divided society in the United States, which has significant repercussions for many different facets of day-to-day life. In addition to the realm of politics, polarization has made its way into social connections, causing tensions to arise between members of the same family, friends, and coworkers who have dissimilar political perspectives. As political identification has become more profound, social networks have been more divided, and there has been a decrease in the inclination to engage in constructive debate.

The landscape of the media has changed as a result of polarization, with conservatives and progressives increasingly gravitating to news sources that coincide with their ideological ideas. Additionally, the media landscape has transformed. Consequently, this pattern has resulted in the construction of media echo chambers, which are environments in which individuals are predominantly exposed to material and points of view that support the ideas they already hold. The information silos that have emerged as a consequence have further contributed to the polarization of political opinion and the destruction of a national narrative that is shared by all.

Cultural Shifts and Identity Politics

The ideological conflict has not been restricted to the arena of politics; rather, it has sparked cultural upheavals and disputes about topics that are tied to identity. The struggle for LGBTQ+ rights, racial justice, gender equality, and immigration policy has resulted in a transformation in the norms and values that are held by society. Questions regarding systematic injustice, historical legacies, and the ever-changing roles of race, gender, and sexuality in American culture have been brought to the forefront as a result of these talks.

There have been considerable achievements made in LGBTQ+ rights, such as the legalization of marriages between people of the same gender and discussions regarding transsexual rights. On the other hand, these modifications have also prompted opposition from conservatives who are skeptical about the rate and scope of LGBTQ+ rights that are being implemented. A national confrontation with institutional racism and past injustices has been sparked as a result of the fight for racial justice, which has been illustrated by demonstrations against police violence and requests for change in criminal justice, respectively.

In the pursuit of gender equality, conventional conventions and roles have been called into question, with topics of discussion ranging from the disparities in income between men and women to reproductive rights and gender identity. In a similar vein, disputes about immigration policy have brought up problems regarding the identity of the nation. Conservatives place a greater emphasis on border security and the preservation of American culture, whilst progressives push for an approach that is more compassionate and inclusive.

The Role of Activism and Social Movements

As a result of the ideological conflict, activism and social movements have emerged on both sides of the split, which has influenced public opinion and the decisions that are made about policy. The Tea Party and the Make America Great Again (MAGA) movement are two examples of grassroots conservative groups that have successfully rallied people to fight for conservative policies and principles. Throughout the course of elections, policy discussions, and the general trajectory of the conservative movement, these movements have been essential in terms of their impact.

Progressive activism has also played a significant role in the process of bringing about change. Movements such as Black Lives Matter, the Women's March, and climate activism have all been essential in bringing attention to issues that are of critical importance. The importance of social justice, equality, and progressive policy reforms has been brought to the forefront as a result of these movements, which have affected policy deliberations.

The ongoing conflict (concluding remarks)

As we get to the end of our investigation of the war of ideas that exists inside American culture, it becomes abundantly evident that this ideological conflict is not even close to being resolved. Its impact extends beyond the field of politics and affects the basic fabric of life being lived in the United States. Even though the collision of ideas has resulted in division, strained social ties, and cultural upheavals, it has also catalyzed progress and a reflection of the nation's growing identity.

The political, social, and cultural destiny of the United States will be influenced by the continuous war for America, which will continue to alter the trajectory of the United States. When Americans are confronted with opposing visions of their nation, they are confronted with basic concerns regarding the role of government, the preservation of individual rights, and the pursuit of a society that is more just and equal.

In the face of this ideological conflict, the capacity to participate in constructive discussion, to bridge differences, and to locate areas of common ground continues to be crucial. The aim is that the collision of ideas will ultimately result in a United States that is more robust, more resilient, and more welcoming to people of all backgrounds, even though differences will continue to exist.

References:

Brookings Institution. (2019). Polarization and Policy: The Impact of Political Polarization in the U.S. Congress. https://www.brookings.edu/research/polarization-and-policy-the-impact-of-political-polarization-in-the-u-s-congress/

Pew Research Center. (2018). Political Polarization in the American Public. https://www.pewresearch.org/politics/2014/06/12/political-polarization-in-the-american-public/

Pew Research Center. (2020). What Unites and Divides Urban, Suburban and Rural Communities. https://www.pewresearch.org/social-trends/2020/05/22/partisan-divides-on-political-values-widen-especially-over-racial-justice-and-immigration/

The Heritage Foundation. (2020). The Tea Party Movement: A Bibliographic Essay. https://www.heritage.org/tea-party/report/the-tea-party-movement-bibliographic-essay

The Washington Post. (2020). How the Black Lives Matter Movement Went Mainstream. https://www.washingtonpost.com/graphics/2020/lifestyle/how-black-lives-matter-shifted-american-politics/

Chapter 6: The Future of America

"THE ROAD AHEAD"

A gloomy prognosis for the future is provided in Chapter 6, which is based on the assumption that extreme leftist elitist parties would attain their goal of establishing a socialist state. It is the purpose of this chapter to investigate the potential repercussions that their objective may have on the economy, national security, and the well-being of society. At the end of the chapter, there is a call to action that encourages the people of the United States to take control of their own destiny and to protect the heritage of the nation for future generations.

Chapter Outline:

1. The Economic Consequences

2. The Impact on National Security

3. The Erosion of Freedom

4. The Decline of Traditional Values

5. The Future of America

6. Conclusion

Part 1: The Economic Consequences

The Shift in Economic Philosophy: The Transition to Socialism

A transition to a socialist state would mark a profound shift in economic philosophy, departing from the principles of capitalism and market-driven economics that have long defined the economic landscape of the United States. To fully appreciate the potential economic consequences of such a transformation, it is essential to delve into the core tenets of socialism and the fundamental differences that distinguish it from capitalism. In this section, we explore the principles of socialism, the implications of state ownership and control, and the complex interplay between these ideological shifts and their economic ramifications.

The Essence of Socialism

Socialism represents a socio-economic system founded on the principles of collective ownership and centralized control over key sectors of the economy. At its core, socialism seeks to address inequalities and disparities in wealth and income through wealth redistribution and government intervention in economic affairs. While various forms of socialism exist, the common thread among them is a departure from private ownership and free-market capitalism.

State ownership and control

One of the most distinctive features of socialism is the transfer of ownership and control from private individuals or entities to the state. In a socialist state, the government owns and controls crucial industries, resources, and means of production. This shift in ownership structure has significant implications for businesses, entrepreneurship, and economic efficiency.

Implications of State Ownership

Reduction in Entrepreneurial Incentives: The transition to state ownership can have a substantial impact on entrepreneurial incentives. The possibility of profit motivates people and businesses in a capitalist system, which promotes innovation, investment, and economic growth. Entrepreneurs take calculated risks with the expectation of reaping the rewards of their endeavors. However, in a socialist state where the government controls major industries, the incentives for entrepreneurship may diminish.

Under socialism, high levels of taxation on businesses and individuals, particularly on high-income earners, are often used as a means of wealth redistribution. While this may address income inequality to some extent, it can also dampen entrepreneurial spirit and risk-taking behavior. Progressive taxation may make people less likely to invest their time, money, and creativity into new businesses or creative projects by limiting the potential rewards of successful ventures.

Furthermore, the state's control over major industries can reduce the opportunities for individuals to launch new enterprises. The barriers to entry into sectors dominated by the government can be substantial, hindering competition and stifling the growth of a dynamic entrepreneurial ecosystem.

Impact on Economic Efficiency: In a socialist economy characterized by state ownership and control, economic efficiency can be compromised. The competitive pressures inherent in a free-market capitalist system are often absent, leading to inefficiencies in resource allocation. Without the motivation to maximize profits and minimize costs, state-owned enterprises may operate with less regard for efficiency and productivity.

Centralized decision-making within government bureaucracies can result in slow response times and suboptimal resource allocation. Unlike market-driven competition, where businesses are driven to continuously improve and innovate to stay competitive, state-owned enterprises may face fewer incentives to enhance their efficiency or adapt to changing consumer preferences.

Additionally, the lack of competition can lead to complacency and reduced accountability within state-owned industries. In the absence of market forces that reward efficiency and innovation, there may be little pressure for these enterprises to improve their performance or provide quality goods and services to consumers.

Wealth Redistribution and Its Implications: Wealth redistribution is a fundamental objective of socialism, aimed at achieving greater income equality and reducing disparities in wealth. Although socialism's proponents hail this objective as a way to address social injustices, it also has significant economic ramifications.

High Taxation on the Wealthy: One of the primary methods of wealth redistribution in socialist systems is the imposition of high tax rates on high-income earners and businesses. The idea behind progressive taxation is to collect a larger share of income from those with higher earnings and redistribute it to support social programs and services.

While the intention may be to promote equity, the effects of high taxation rates on the wealthy can extend beyond the redistribution of wealth. High-income individuals and businesses may respond to elevated tax rates by altering their behavior and financial strategies. These responses can have wide-ranging economic consequences.

Tax Avoidance: High-income individuals may engage in tax avoidance strategies, such as offshore investments, deductions, and credits, to reduce their tax liabilities. This can result in reduced tax revenue for the government, potentially necessitating higher tax rates for the wealthy to maintain revenue streams.

Reduced Investment: Elevated taxes on businesses can discourage investment in capital, equipment, and expansion. When businesses face higher costs due to taxation, they may limit their capital expenditures, leading to slower economic growth and reduced job creation.

Incentive Effects: High taxation can affect the incentives for work, savings, and investment. People might be less motivated to work longer hours or pursue higher-paying opportunities if taxation reduces the potential rewards of earning additional income. Similarly, the incentives to save and invest may be reduced, impacting capital formation.

Economic Growth: The cumulative impact of reduced investment, altered behavior, and disincentives to work can influence overall economic growth. Lower economic growth rates can hinder job creation, limit wage growth, and lead to stagnation in the standard of living.

Navigating the Economic Terrain

The shift in economic philosophy from capitalism to socialism entails a fundamental transformation in the ownership and control of key industries, as well as a reimagining of wealth redistribution policies. While socialism seeks to address income inequality and promote social welfare, it also raises complex economic challenges.

Navigating the economic terrain of socialism requires careful consideration of trade-offs. Balancing the objectives of wealth redistribution with economic efficiency, innovation, and incentives is a multifaceted endeavor. In the chapters that follow, we will continue to explore the potential consequences of a socialist state on various aspects of American society, including national security, societal well-being, and the imperative of safeguarding the nation's heritage for future generations.

Challenges in Resource Allocation

One of the central challenges in a socialist system lies in resource allocation. Unlike market-driven economies, where supply and demand dictate resource distribution, socialism relies on central planning and government control to make these critical decisions. In this section, we will delve deeper into the intricacies of resource allocation in socialist economies, exploring the concept of central planning, the consequences of misallocation, and the potential for shortages and surpluses.

Central Planning: The Backbone of Socialist Resource Allocation

Central planning is a hallmark of socialist economies, serving as the mechanism through which resources are allocated, production targets are set, and economic decisions are made. The fundamental idea behind central planning is to replace the decentralized decision-making of a free-market system with a central authority responsible for coordinating economic activities.

Central Planners and Decision-Making

Under socialism, central planners, often government officials or bureaucrats, play a pivotal role in determining what goods and services should be produced, how they should be produced, and in what quantities. These decisions are based on various factors, including social priorities, political considerations, and the pursuit of economic equality.

The Information Challenge

Central planning faces a significant challenge: the gathering and processing of vast amounts of information. In a complex economy, information about consumer preferences, production costs, technological advancements, and resource availability is distributed among countless individuals, businesses, and industries. Collecting and analyzing this information comprehensively is a formidable task.

Resource Allocation Models

To address the information challenge, central planners often rely on resource allocation models. These models attempt to simulate economic conditions, allowing planners to make informed decisions. These models, however, may find it difficult to take into account the complexities of real-world situations because of their inherent limitations and simplifications.

Misallocation of resources

One of the critical concerns in socialist resource allocation is the potential for misallocation. When central planners make decisions about production and resource allocation, there is a risk that their choices may not align with actual consumer preferences or market demand.

Consumer Sovereignty

In market-driven economies, consumer sovereignty is a guiding principle. It emphasizes that consumers, through their choices and purchasing decisions, influence which goods and services are produced and in what quantities. This mechanism ensures that resources are allocated in a way that aligns with consumer demand.

In a socialist system, however, consumer preferences may not hold the same sway. Central planners, guided by other considerations, may allocate resources to industries or products that do not necessarily align with what consumers desire. This misalignment can result in an oversupply of certain goods and services and an undersupply of others.

Shortages and surpluses

One of the most tangible consequences of misallocation under socialism is the emergence of shortages and surpluses. These imbalances can have a direct impact on the availability of essential goods and services, affecting the daily lives of citizens.

Shortages

Shortages occur when the demand for a particular product or service exceeds its supply. In a socialist system, shortages can manifest due to several reasons:

Inaccurate Planning: Central planners may underestimate consumer demand, leading to insufficient production levels.

Bureaucratic Delays: Administrative hurdles and bureaucratic inefficiencies can slow down the production and distribution of goods, exacerbating shortages.

Resource Constraints: Limited access to resources, raw materials, or production inputs can impede the production of certain goods, resulting in shortages.

Shortages can lead to frustration, inconvenience, and even the rationing of essential items. Citizens may find it difficult to access goods like food, medicine, or fuel, leading to long queues and frustration.

Surpluses

Conversely, surpluses occur when the supply of a product exceeds demand, leading to an excess of unsold goods. Surpluses can be problematic for several reasons:

Wasted Resources: Excessive production consumes resources and labor that could have been allocated more efficiently elsewhere.

Storage Costs: Maintaining surpluses incurs storage and holding costs for the government, potentially straining budgets.

Lack of Innovation: Surpluses can disincentivize producers from innovating or improving their products, as there is little competitive pressure.

Central Planning and Resource Allocation: A Delicate Balancing Act

Central planning in socialist economies represents a complex and delicate balancing act. While it seeks to address inequality and ensure that essential goods and services are accessible to all citizens, it faces inherent challenges in information processing, decision-making, and resource allocation.

Efforts to improve the efficiency of central planning have been ongoing, with some socialist countries experimenting with elements of market-oriented reforms. These reforms aim to introduce market mechanisms to socialist systems, allowing for more responsive resource allocation while preserving socialist principles.

Global Impact of a Socialist United States: Economic, Diplomatic, and Geopolitical Ramifications

The prospect of the United States adopting socialism as its governing ideology carries profound implications not only for the nation itself but also for the international community. Such a transformation would ripple through the global landscape, influencing economic dynamics, reshaping diplomatic relations, and redefining the geopolitical order. In this section, we will explore the potential global impact of a socialist United States, shedding light on the intricate web of consequences that could unfold.

Economic Ramifications

Disruption of the Global Economic Order: The United States, as the world's largest economy, wields substantial influence over the global economic order. A shift towards socialism would disrupt this order in several ways:

Trade and Investment: The U.S. has historically championed free trade and market-oriented economic policies. A move towards socialism could lead to protectionist measures, trade restrictions, and reduced openness to foreign investment, creating uncertainty in global markets.

Global Supply Chains: Many multinational corporations have intricate global supply chains that rely on the free flow of goods and services. A socialist U.S. might introduce trade barriers and regulations that disrupt these supply chains, impacting industries worldwide.

Currency Markets: The U.S. dollar serves as the world's primary reserve currency. Any economic upheaval in the U.S. could affect the stability of global currency markets and international financial systems.

Investor Confidence: International investors often view the U.S. as a safe haven for their capital. A shift towards socialism may erode investor confidence, leading to capital flight and volatility in global financial markets.

Impact on Developing Economies

Developing economies often depend on trade with the United States for economic growth and stability. A socialist U.S. may reduce its engagement with these nations, impacting their exports and economic prospects. Additionally, reduced foreign aid and assistance could affect vulnerable populations in developing countries.

Diplomatic Relations

Shifting alliances and partnerships: The diplomatic landscape would undergo significant realignments if the U.S. embraced socialism.

Alliances: Long-standing military and strategic alliances, such as NATO, could be reevaluated. Socialist policies may lead to decreased defense spending or shifts in military priorities, potentially straining relationships with traditional allies.

Regional Powers: Socialist principles might lead to a re-evaluation of relationships with regional powers like China and Russia. Cooperation or conflict could intensify, depending on the U.S.'s stance on key issues.

Diplomatic Initiatives: The U.S. often plays a central role in diplomatic initiatives worldwide. A shift towards socialism could alter its approach to international conflicts, peace negotiations, and humanitarian efforts.

Trade agreements and alliances

Trade agreements, which are essential for economic prosperity and global integration, could be affected.

Existing Agreements: The U.S. may reconsider its participation in existing trade agreements, potentially leading to renegotiations or withdrawals, which could impact global trade dynamics.

New Trade Partners: Socialist policies might lead the U.S. to seek new trade partners with similar ideologies, potentially shifting trade routes and alliances.

Geopolitical Ramifications

Global Power Dynamics: The rise of socialism in the U.S. could reshape the global power balance.

China's Ascendancy: China, with its socialist-oriented system, might seize the opportunity to expand its influence and challenge the U.S. as the world's preeminent superpower.

Deterioration of Soft Power: The U.S. has long wielded soft power through its democratic values, culture, and institutions. A socialist turn could weaken this soft power, impacting its ability to shape global narratives and influence other nations.

International Responses

The response of other nations to a socialist United States would be multifaceted:

Economic Responses: Countries may adjust their economic policies in response to changes in U.S. economic behavior. Trade restrictions, currency adjustments, and investment decisions could all come into play.

Diplomatic Realignments: Nations may reassess their diplomatic priorities and alliances in light of U.S. policy changes, leading to shifts in global diplomatic dynamics.

Global Governance: The role of the U.S. in international organizations and global governance structures could evolve, potentially impacting the effectiveness and legitimacy of these institutions.

Conclusion: Navigating Uncertain Waters

There has been a great deal of discussion and worry on the possible economic repercussions that may result from a socialist change at the United States level. While those who support it claim that it has the potential to solve issues of social injustice and income inequality, those who oppose it express legitimate worries about the impact it will have on entrepreneurship, innovation, resource allocation, and the capacity to maintain budgetary sustainability.

Having a deep grasp of the trade-offs that are involved is necessary in order to successfully navigate the murky seas of economic transition. Maintaining a healthy equilibrium between social welfare, economic incentives, and efficiency is a challenging endeavor. To determine the nation's economic trajectory in the years to come, politicians, residents, and leaders must engage in conversations that are both educated and productive.

The route that lies ahead is riddled with difficulties and ambiguities, but it is a path that the people of the United States of America must collaboratively construct. In the next chapters, we will investigate the potential repercussions that socialist policies might have on the nation's security, the well-being of society, and the necessity of preserving the nation's legacy for the generations who will come after us.

References:

Piketty, T. (2014). Capital in the Twenty-First Century. Harvard University Press.

Smith, A. (1776). An Inquiry into the Nature and Causes of the Wealth of Nations. London: W. Strahan and T. Cadell.

Hayek, F. A. (1945). The Use of Knowledge in Society. The American Economic Review, 35(4), 519-530.

Keynes, J. M. (1936). The General Theory of Employment, Interest and Money. Macmillan.

Part 2: The Impact on National Security

The intersection of socialism and national security is a multifaceted and often contentious terrain. In this part, we will begin an in-depth investigation of how the implementation of socialist ideals in the United States may have an impact on the country's national security situation. As part of our discussion, we will go into important topics such as defense budget, military preparedness, strategic alliances, intelligence capabilities, and the larger ramifications for the stability of the global community.

Defense Spending and Resource Allocation

Redefining Priorities: One of the most immediate and consequential impacts of socialism on national security would be a potential shift in defense spending and resource allocation. People who adhere to socialist ideas frequently emphasize domestic welfare programs, economic redistribution, and social services, all of which have the potential to compete with the military for financing.

Historical Perspective: Historically, socialist-leaning governments have, at times, reduced defense spending to divert resources to social programs. One school of thought contends that this might potentially weaken a nation's ability to respond to security concerns, while another school of thought maintains that it could potentially generate stronger internal stability.

Military Modernization: Maintaining a modern, technologically advanced military requires significant investment. Attempts to modernize the military might be hampered by reductions in defense spending, which could potentially make the armed forces less capable of responding to new threats.

Impact on Military Personnel

A socialist shift could also affect the composition and size of the military workforce:

Personnel Reductions: To allocate resources to social programs, a socialist government might consider reducing the size of the armed forces, which could have implications for national defense capabilities.

Quality vs. Quantity: A shift towards a smaller, more technologically advanced military may prioritize quality over quantity. This may result in a military force that is smaller but more highly skilled.

Military Readiness and Preparedness

Training and Exercises: Military readiness is a cornerstone of national security. It takes into account a wide variety of aspects, including as training, the upkeep of equipment, and strategic planning. Socialism may have a substantial influence on these areas:

Training: Adequate training is essential for military effectiveness. As a result of reduced military resources, the frequency and breadth of training exercises may be restricted, which may result in a subsequent decrease in readiness levels.

Maintenance: Proper maintenance of military equipment is crucial. Constraints on the budget might make it difficult to maintain and improve armament, which would have a negative influence on the efficacy of the fight.

Strategic Readiness: A socialist government may place different priorities on military readiness, potentially shifting the focus from traditional defense to non-traditional security challenges, such as cyber warfare or humanitarian missions.

Strategic Alliances and International Relations

Shifting Alliances: The United States' international alliances are a cornerstone of its national security strategy. There is a possibility that a socialist shift may force re-evaluations of certain alignments:

Traditional Allies: Traditional military allies, such as NATO member countries, may question the U.S.'s commitment to collective defense if defense spending is reduced or strategic priorities change.

Regional Partnerships: Socialist principles may lead the U.S. to strengthen diplomatic and military ties with like-minded nations, potentially reshaping regional security dynamics.

Global Stability

The broader implications of a socialist United States on global stability cannot be overlooked:

Power Vacuum: A decline in the capabilities of the United States military or a shift in priorities might generate a perceived power vacuum, which would invite aggressive responses from adversaries or regional powers.

Conflict Resolution: The U.S. often plays a pivotal role in global conflict resolution and peacekeeping efforts. It is possible that a socialist administration would place greater emphasis on diplomacy and international collaboration, which might potentially change the way that global disputes are resolved.

Intelligence Capabilities and Cybersecurity

Intelligence Gathering: Capabilities that are effective in gathering intelligence are essential for the protection of the nation. A socialist administration might reorder the priorities of intelligence:

Cyber Threats: In an increasingly digital world, the focus on cybersecurity and cyber intelligence may grow. increase investment in this sector.

Emphasis on Domestic Threats: Socialist governments may prioritize monitoring and addressing domestic security threats, potentially reallocating intelligence resources from international to domestic concerns.

Information Sharing: International intelligence cooperation is a linchpin of global security. These collaborations might be impacted by shifts in the priorities or capabilities of the United States intelligence community:

Information Sharing: Socialist principles may lead to greater emphasis on international information sharing and collaboration on security matters.

Trust and Confidentiality: Balancing intelligence sharing with concerns about trust and confidentiality could become more complex under a socialist government.

Conclusion: Navigating a Complex Landscape

The effect that socialism has on national security is a complex matter that can have repercussions for a variety of aspects, including defense budget, military readiness, strategic alliances, intelligence capabilities, and global stability. Proponents of socialist ideas believe that they can help to create internal stability and emphasize non-traditional security concerns. On the other hand, detractors claim that these values may damage a nation's ability to successfully react to security threats.

It would be necessary to do a careful balancing act to successfully navigate this complicated terrain. This would involve ensuring that the nation's security interests are protected while also addressing domestic needs. It would be necessary for the United States to modify its national security policy to align it with the ideological change. This might result in the modification of the United States' role in the world as well as its approach to international relations.

We will dig into additional important issues as we continue our investigation into the potential repercussions of a socialist United States of America. These aspects include the influence on the well-being of society, the preservation of national history, and the necessity of ensuring the future of the nation for future generations.

References:

Smith, A. (1776). An Inquiry into the Nature and Causes of the Wealth of Nations. London: W. Strahan and T. Cadell.

Hayek, F. A. (1945). The Use of Knowledge in Society. The American Economic Review, 35(4), 519-530.

Keynes, J. M. (1936). The General Theory of Employment, Interest and Money. Macmillan.

Part 3: The Erosion of Freedom

In our exploration of the potential consequences of a socialist United States, we turn our attention to a fundamental concern—the erosion of individual freedoms and liberties. The clash between collectivist ideologies and personal freedoms has long been a central issue in political discourse. In this section, we will embark on a comprehensive analysis of how socialism might affect various aspects of individual liberty, ranging from free speech to property rights, while also delving into the distinctive characteristics of Marxist regimes and their utilization of the state as a weapon against their own people.

Freedom of speech and expression

The Role of State Control: One of the most critical aspects of individual freedom is the right to free speech and expression. In a socialist framework, the role of the state in controlling and regulating speech can become a contentious issue.

Media Ownership: Socialist governments may advocate for state ownership or heavy regulation of media outlets, potentially limiting diverse voices and viewpoints in the public sphere.

Censorship: Concerns about censorship may arise with the state exercising control over content deemed contrary to socialist ideology. This can curtail political dissent and free expression.

Marxist Influence: Marxist regimes, in particular, have a history of tightly controlling the media and suppressing dissenting voices. They view the media as a tool for advancing the ideology of the ruling class, effectively weaponizing it against those who oppose their rule.

Balancing rights and responsibilities

Socialism often emphasizes the collective good over individual rights. Balancing the right to free expression with responsibilities to the collective can be challenging.

Hate Speech: Socialist governments may take a stricter stance on hate speech and incitement, potentially limiting certain forms of expression to maintain social harmony.

Political Dissent: The suppression of political dissent may become a contentious issue, with governments justifying restrictions on the grounds of protecting the socialist agenda.

Marxist Coercion: Marxist states have historically silenced dissidents through intimidation, imprisonment, or even violence. They view any form of dissent as a threat to their control and are willing to use the state's power to quell opposition.

Property Rights and Economic Freedom

Redistribution of wealth: One of the defining features of socialism is the redistribution of wealth. This can have profound implications for property rights and economic freedom.

Property Ownership: Socialist policies may lead to increased state ownership of key industries and assets, potentially limiting private property rights.

Income Redistribution: The progressive taxation systems often associated with socialism may result in substantial wealth redistribution, impacting economic freedom.

Marxist Seizure: In Marxist regimes, the state often seizes private property and means of production, with the goal of abolishing private property altogether. This can lead to the confiscation of assets and the elimination of economic freedoms.

Regulatory Measures

Socialist governments often implement regulatory measures to control economic activity. These regulations can affect entrepreneurial freedom:

Business Regulations: Increased regulations on businesses can limit entrepreneurial freedom and innovation, potentially stifling economic growth.

Price Controls: Price controls may be imposed on certain goods and services, affecting market dynamics and individual economic choices.

Marxist Central Planning: Marxist states are known for central planning, where the state dictates economic decisions and resource allocation. This centralized control leaves little room for economic freedom and innovation.

Individual autonomy vs. collective responsibility

Navigating the Balance: A central challenge in a socialist society is navigating the balance between individual autonomy and collective responsibility.

Social Safety Nets: Socialist policies often aim to provide robust social safety nets. While this can enhance individual well-being, it may also reduce the incentive for personal responsibility.

State Intervention: Extensive state intervention in various aspects of life, from education to healthcare, can limit individual choices and decision-making.

Marxist Ideology: Marxist states, driven by the ideology of class struggle and historical materialism, prioritize the interests of the proletariat over individual rights. They argue that the state's control is necessary to achieve the ultimate goal of a classless society.

The Role of Civil Liberties

Privacy and surveillance: Civil liberties, including privacy and protection from unwarranted surveillance, are integral to individual freedom.

Surveillance State: Socialist governments may expand surveillance capabilities in the name of national security, potentially infringing on privacy rights.

Digital Privacy: The collection and analysis of digital data can raise concerns about privacy and personal freedoms in a socialist context.

Marxist Totalitarianism: Marxist regimes often employ extensive surveillance to monitor citizens' activities and suppress dissent. This level of surveillance infringes on individual liberties and creates an atmosphere of fear and mistrust.

Conclusion: Balancing Ideals and Liberties

The potential erosion of individual freedoms and liberties in a socialist United States is a deeply complex issue, characterized by a delicate balancing act between collective ideals and personal autonomy. While proponents argue that socialist policies can enhance social justice and reduce inequality, critics contend that they may come at the cost of individual liberties.

Navigating this terrain would require thoughtful consideration of the trade-offs between collective responsibility and personal freedoms. Striking a balance that preserves individual rights while advancing societal welfare is a challenge that transcends ideological boundaries. Furthermore, understanding the distinct characteristics of Marxist regimes and their use of the state as a weapon against their own people is essential in assessing the potential consequences of socialist governance. As we continue our exploration of the consequences of a socialist America, we will delve into additional critical aspects, including the implications for the economy, national security, and the imperative of safeguarding the nation's heritage for future generations.

References:

Rawls, J. (1971). A Theory of Justice. Harvard University Press.

Locke, J. (1689). Two Treatises of Government. A. Millar, J. and R. Tonson, H. Woodfall, J. Rivington, et al.

Bellah, R. N., Madsen, R., Sullivan, W. M., Swidler, A., & Tipton, S. M. (1985). Habits of the Heart: Individualism and Commitment in American Life. University of California Press.

Marx, K., & Engels, F. (1848). The Communist Manifesto. London: League of the Just.

Part 4: The Decline of Traditional Values

As we proceed with our investigation into the probable repercussions of a socialist United States, we will now focus on an essential facet, which is the deterioration of traditional values. Societies are shaped in large part by the cultural norms, moral ideals, and social traditions that exist inside people. In the next part, we will perform a comprehensive examination of the ways in which socialism may have an effect on traditional values, as well as investigate the many methods that Marxist governments have utilized to undermine these values.

The Role of Cultural Norms

Traditional Values and Their Significance: There is a vast variety of ideas and behaviors that have been handed down from generation to generation that are included in the category of traditional values. Family values, religious beliefs, personal accountability, and ethical standards are frequently included in these concepts. The identity of many civilizations, including that of the United States of America, has been significantly influenced by these ideals, which in turn have played a foundational role.

Family Values: Traditional family structures have been a cornerstone of American culture for a long time. These structures emphasize the significance of marriage, parental duties, and the stability of the family unit.

Religious Beliefs: The United States has a long history of religious freedom and pluralism, with religious values influencing both personal ethics and public policies.

Moral Ethics: Traditional values have emphasized principles such as honesty, integrity, and personal responsibility.

Socialist Critique

Socialist ideologies often challenge traditional values on several fronts:

Family and Class Struggle: Marxist theory views the family as a product of class struggle and often advocates for the dissolution of traditional family structures. Marxists contend that the family is a mechanism that the bourgeoisie uses to keep power and that it is responsible for the perpetuation of inequality.

Religion and Ideology: Socialist regimes, particularly of the Marxist variety, may perceive religion as a threat to their ideology. To accomplish their goal of establishing a society without social classes, they would try to restrict religious activities and encourage atheism.

Moral Relativism: Socialist ideologies sometimes embrace moral relativism, suggesting that traditional moral values are a product of social conditioning and can be discarded in favor of collective values.

The Impact of Socialist Policies

The Roles of Families and Genders: Socialist policies can bring about significant changes in family dynamics and gender roles:

State Intervention in Child Rearing: Socialist governments may expand their role in child-rearing, providing state-funded childcare and education. The traditional role of the family in the raising of children may be diminished as a result of this, although it can be beneficial to working parents.

Gender Equality: Socialist policies often emphasize gender equality, aiming to eliminate disparities in employment and domestic roles. Even though this may be beneficial to women's rights, it may also pose a threat to conventional gender norms.

Religious Freedom and Persecution

The relationship between socialism and religion can be complex:

Religious Freedom: Socialist states may guarantee religious freedom in theory, but in practice, they may restrict religious practices and limit the influence of religious institutions.

Religious Persecution: Marxist regimes, in particular, have a history of religious persecution. As a result of their perception that religion poses a possible danger to their ideology, they have chosen to repress religious organizations and behaviors.

Moral Values and Education

Socialist governments often exert control over education, influencing the moral values imparted to future generations:

State-Driven Education: Socialist states may centralize education systems, allowing them to shape curricula and promote values aligned with their ideology.

Marxist Indoctrination: Marxist regimes have used education as a means of indoctrinating young minds with their ideology, often portraying traditional values as regressive and incompatible with their vision of a classless society.

The Marxist Assault on Traditional Values

To dismantle conventional values and rearrange cultural norms, Marxist governments employ a variety of unique techniques, including the following:

Cultural Revolution: Marxist revolutions, such as Mao's Cultural Revolution in China, have attempted to abolish traditional culture and values via the use of public campaigns, purges, and re-education for the masses.

State Control of Media: Marxists often establish strict control over media outlets, using them to disseminate propaganda and reshape cultural narratives to align with their ideology.

Suppression of Dissent: Marxist states frequently suppress dissent and cultural expressions that deviate from the official ideology. People who are intellectuals, authors, and artists are frequently the targets of censorship and threats of persecution.

The Dilemma of Cultural Transformation

The potential transformation of cultural norms and values in a socialist America raises a profound dilemma. Proponents of socialist policies say that they have the potential to advance social justice and equality, while detractors claim that they may weaken the cultural roots that have been the driving force behind the formation of American society for a very long time.

To successfully navigate this terrain, it would be necessary to give serious thought to the trade-offs that exist between the advancement of society and the protection of cultural assets. Striking a balance that acknowledges the importance of cultural variety and individual liberties while also tackling the issue of systematic inequality is a difficult problem.

Conclusion: Cultural Evolution or Devolution

The potential decline of traditional values in a socialist United States is a multifaceted issue with far-reaching consequences. The clash between socialist ideologies and traditional cultural norms creates a tension that must be addressed with sensitivity and nuance.

Furthermore, understanding the distinct strategies employed by Marxist regimes in dismantling traditional values is essential in assessing the potential consequences of socialist governance. The history of Marxist revolutions provides valuable insights into the methods and tactics they employ to reshape societies.

As we continue our exploration of the consequences of a socialist America, we will delve into additional critical aspects, including the implications for the economy, national security, and the imperative of safeguarding the nation's heritage for future generations.

References:

Rawls, J. (1971). A Theory of Justice. Harvard University Press.

Locke, J. (1689). Two Treatises of Government. A. Millar, J. and R. Tonson, H. Woodfall, J. Rivington, et al.

Bellah, R. N., Madsen, R., Sullivan, W. M., Swidler, A., & Tipton, S. M. (1985). Habits of the Heart: Individualism and Commitment in American Life. University of California Press.

Marx, K., & Engels, F. (1848). The Communist Manifesto. London: League of the Just.

Part 5. The Future of America

There is a complicated and controversial discourse around socialism and its implications for the future of the United States of America. This discourse frequently divides public opinion and provokes discussion among academics. In its most fundamental form, socialism may be understood as an economic and political philosophy that advocates for the ownership and administration of the means of production and distribution of products by a collective or governmental entity. This philosophy tries to solve concerns of economic inequality and social injustice by advocating for the distribution of wealth, the establishment of social welfare programs, and the abolition of class hierarchies. On the other hand, socialism is not a singular ideology; rather, it covers a wide range of distinct ideas, ranging from democratic socialism to more extreme variants, such as Marxism.

A criticism of capitalism that is centered on the idea of class struggle is presented by Marxism, which is a form of socialism that was created in the 19th century by Karl Marx and Friedrich Engels. It is the contention of Marxists that capitalism fundamentally exploits the working class, also known as the proletariat, for the advantage of the owning class, also known as the bourgeoisie, which results in social and economic inequality. They call for the revolutionary destruction of capitalism systems in order to initiate the establishment of a society without classes in which resources and power are divided in an equitable manner. Marxists sometimes highlight the necessity for drastic change, sometimes by revolutionary methods, in contrast to democratic socialists, who aim to accomplish their goals through progressive reform within existing political structures. Marxists may also aspire to achieve their goals through revolutionary means.

It is important to investigate the possible influence that socialism, and Marxism in particular, might have on the future of the United States of America for a number of reasons. First and foremost, it makes it possible to conduct an in-depth analysis of the present economic and social difficulties that the United States of America is facing, such as the disparity in income, the accessibility of healthcare, and the rights of workers. In the second place, it offers a perspective that may be utilized to contemplate alternative models of economic organization and governance that have the potential to address these challenges. Thirdly, the dispute between socialism and capitalism focuses on basic values and concepts, such as freedom, equality, and the role that the government plays in the lives of individuals.

On top of that, the conversation is quite current. There has been a resurgence of interest in socialist ideals among some elements of the American people, particularly among younger generations, in recent years. This interest has been particularly prevalent among younger generations. This transition is a reflection of rising worries about the viability of existing economic arrangements as well as the desire for a society that is more equal. On the other hand, it has also aroused great discussion and worry among many who believe that socialism, and Marxism in particular, is incompatible with American principles and as destructive to economic success and individual liberties.

In light of these factors, the investigation of the possible effects that socialism may have on the United States of America is not only an intellectual exercise; rather, it is an essential engagement with matters about the path that the nation will take in the future. It encourages a contemplative examination of the ways in which various ideologies may make policies, have an impact on cultural values, and have an impact on the lives of individuals in their day-to-day lives. In light of the fact that the United States of America is currently at a crossroads, it is essential to investigate the repercussions of adopting or rejecting socialist ideals in order to influence public discourse and policy decisions that will have an impact on the nation for many generations to come.

The Divisive Strategies of Marxist Regimes

Class Struggle as a Tool: Marxist ideology is fundamentally rooted in the concept of class struggle. This ideology is used as a tactic by Marxist governments to divide societies:

Marxist nations frequently exacerbate class tensions by presenting the bourgeoisie as oppressors and the proletariat as the downtrodden. This is referred to as class warfare. It is because of this that various socioeconomic groups develop feelings of animosity and enmity toward one another.

Political and economic polarization may occur when Marxist governments enact policies that worsen existing economic inequities, so widening the gap between those who are rich and those who are less well off.

Identity Politics: Marxist governments may promote identity politics, which emphasizes distinctions based on race, gender, or other criteria, as a tactic to foment division and divert from economic difficulties. This is done to capitalize on the fact that these disparities exist.

Suppression of Dissent, Marxist regimes have a history of suppressing dissent and silencing opposition:

Censorship: Marxist regimes frequently exert control over the media and communication networks, which limits the distribution of points of view that are contrary to the governments.

Political Persecution: Dissidents, activists, and intellectuals who challenge the Marxist ideology may face imprisonment, exile, or even violence.

State Surveillance: Extensive surveillance apparatuses are used to monitor citizens, creating an atmosphere of fear and self-censorship.

Economic Consequences

The Impact on Prosperity, a shift toward socialism may have substantial ramifications for the economy, including the following:
The redistribution of wealth: Policies that are designed to redistribute money have the potential to impede innovation and

entrepreneurialism, which might ultimately result in economic stagnation.

Central Planning: Marxist regimes often implement central planning, which can result in inefficiencies and resource misallocation.

Foreign Investment: A socialist America may deter foreign investment, impacting economic growth and job creation.

The Dilemma of Economic Equality; while socialism aims to address economic inequalities, the pursuit of economic equality can have unintended consequences:

Incentive Reduction: High taxes and wealth redistribution may reduce the incentive for individuals and businesses to excel and innovate.

Economic Stagnation: Excessive government control can lead to economic stagnation, as central planning may not efficiently allocate resources.

Market Distortion: Socialist policies can distort market dynamics, potentially leading to shortages and surpluses.

National Security Concerns

Weakening of Defense and National security is a critical concern, and socialist policies can affect a nation's defense capabilities:
Defense Budget: A socialist government may prioritize social programs over defense spending, potentially weakening the military.

Foreign Relations: Ideological differences between socialist and non-socialist states can strain diplomatic relations and alliances.

Military Strength: A decline in defense spending can lead to a reduction in military capabilities, impacting a nation's ability to protect its interests.

The Role of Cultural Transformation

Impact on Cultural Identity. Cultural norms and values are an integral part of a nation's identity. Socialist policies can reshape cultural narratives:

Cultural Revolution: Marxist regimes may initiate cultural revolutions to erase traditional values and promote ideological conformity.

Censorship of Arts: Creative expression, including literature and the arts, may be subject to censorship if it conflicts with socialist ideology.

Suppression of Religion: Religious practices and institutions may be suppressed, leading to a decline in cultural diversity.

The Imperative of Safeguarding Heritage

In the face of these potential challenges, safeguarding the heritage of the nation for future generations becomes imperative. Preserving cultural traditions, individual freedoms, and economic opportunities is essential to ensure a prosperous and united future.

Conclusion: A Critical Crossroads

The future of America stands at a critical crossroads, where the path towards socialism, particularly of the Marxist variety, raises profound questions about the nation's destiny. The intricacy of this ideological transition is shown by the techniques that Marxist governments have utilized to erode the foundations of society and split it within itself.

As we come to the end of our investigation into the potential repercussions of a socialist America, it is abundantly evident that the decisions that are taken in the areas of economics, national security, and cultural values will have a significant influence on the legacy that is handed down to subsequent generations. Maintaining a steady equilibrium between the pursuit of social justice and the protection of individual rights and cultural variety continues to be a tremendous obstacle, one that calls for careful thinking and concerted effort from all parties involved.

References:

Bellah, R. N., Madsen, R., Sullivan, W. M., Swidler, A., & Tipton, S. M. (1985). Habits of the Heart: Individualism and Commitment in American Life. University of California Press.

Hayek, F. A. (1945). The Use of Knowledge in Society. The American Economic Review, 35(4), 519-530.

Keynes, J. M. (1936). The General Theory of Employment, Interest and Money. Macmillan.

Locke, J. (1689). Two Treatises of Government. A. Millar, J. and R. Tonson, H. Woodfall, J. Rivington, et al.

Marx, K., & Engels, F. (1848). The Communist Manifesto. London: League of the Just.

Piketty, T. (2014). Capital in the Twenty-First Century. Harvard University Press.

Rawls, J. (1971). A Theory of Justice. Harvard University Press.

Smith, A. (1776). An Inquiry into the Nature and Causes of the Wealth of Nations. London: W. Strahan and T. Cadell.

Conclusion: Shaping the Destiny of a Nation

Within the pages of this book, we have gone on a profound trip through the complex web of ideologies, politics, and societal factors that will determine the destiny of the United States of America. As we come to the end of our investigation into the path that lies ahead, it is imperative that we take some time to contemplate the crucial intersection at which the nation currently finds itself. There is a significant possibility that radical leftist elitist parties may be successful in attaining their objective of building a socialist state, which casts a shadow of doubt and uncertainty over the future of the nation. In this all-encompassing conclusion, we will summarize the most important takeaways from our study and deliver a thundering call to action for the people of the United States of America.

The Intersection of Ideologies

Our voyage started with a glimpse into the core of a strong ideological conflict. It was an epic war between those who advocated for socialism, particularly of the Marxist sort, and others who were determined to maintain the traditional values and foundations upon which the United States of America was established. We were witnesses to the war of ideas, as well as the techniques that Marxist governments utilized in order to split American society, damage its economic foundations, and modify cultural standards. At this crucial stage, it is very necessary to take into consideration the far-reaching consequences that will result from the decisions that are to come.

Safeguarding Heritage for Future Generations

There is no such thing as a choice when it comes to the preservation of a nation's legacy; rather, it is an impossible necessity. It necessitates a subtle balance, which is a combination of the pursuit of social justice with the protection of individual rights, economic opportunity, and the kaleidoscope of cultural variety that distinguishes the United States of America. This delicate balancing act requires a commitment to uphold the principles upon which the nation was founded while addressing genuine concerns of social inequality and injustice.

The Role of Civic Engagement

It is not the case that political elites or ideological movements have predetermined the destiny of the United States of America. On the contrary, it is in the hands of the people who live there. Civic engagement, informed discourse, and active participation in the democratic process constitute the very essence of safeguarding the nation's legacy. It is possible for the United States of America to successfully traverse the complex maze that is today's 21st century if they engage in constructive discourse, make concessions, and work toward achieving common goals.

Charting a Course Forward

As we conclude this profound exploration of the road ahead, a resounding call to action reverberates throughout the land—a call for Americans to seize control of their destiny, shield the nation's heritage, and shape a future that harmonizes with the nation's most cherished traditions and loftiest aspirations.

Neither the difficulties that are presented by the possibility of socialism are insurmountable nor are they insurmountable as well. They are, instead, an invitation for the nation to join in a vigorous conversation about its future, to innovate and adapt to changing circumstances, and to reaffirm its uncompromising adherence to the ideals of liberty, democracy, and individual rights.

In the chapters that came before this conclusion, we were able to observe the complex interaction of ideologies, the collision of ideas, and the potential repercussions that may result from the decisions that we were going to make. The path that lies ahead is accompanied by a cloud of uncertainty; but it is also lighted by the possibilities that the resiliency of the United States of America and its steadfast dedication to its fundamental principles may bring about.

The Destiny of America: A Collective Responsibility

America's future is not in the hands of a single leader or a single political party; rather, it is in the hands of its people. As we move forward, the destiny of the nation will ultimately be determined by the vision, perseverance, and commitment of the American people. This will be the case as we navigate the way forward. In terms of democracy and self-governance, the United States of America is a tremendous experiment that is still unfolding. It is sure that the decisions that are taken in the days, months, and years to follow will reverberate through the ages and leave their mark on the annals of history.

Conclusion: A Beacon of Hope

It is imperative that we understand that the path that lies ahead may be riddled with difficulties and uncertainties, but it is also a demonstration of the unyielding spirit that is the United States of America. Through the years, the nation has endured storms, triumphed over divides, and developed into what it is today. across the course of its existence, it has served as a light of hope, a symbol of independence, and a source of inspiration for a great number of people all across the world.

As we proceed with our investigation into the future of the United States of America, let us not forget that it is not the difficulties we encounter that define us, but rather how we react to those difficulties. In the hands of its people, the United States of America have the potential to design a future that represents the principles upon which it was founded—a future in which liberty, justice, and prosperity are all available to everyone. The destiny of a nation is a collaborative undertaking.

Our trip through the complex web of American culture, politics, and ideas has come to an end with this conclusion. In the process of navigating the unknown seas of the 21st century, may the insights obtained serve as a compass for the nation, allowing it to chart a route toward a future that honors the heritage of the past while also building a path of growth and hope for future generations.

References:

Bellah, R. N., Madsen, R., Sullivan, W. M., Swidler, A., & Tipton, S. M. (1985). Habits of the Heart: Individualism and Commitment in American Life. University of California Press.

Hayek, F. A. (1945). The Use of Knowledge in Society. The American Economic Review, 35(4), 519-530.

Keynes, J. M. (1936). The General Theory of Employment, Interest and Money. Macmillan.

Locke, J. (1689). Two Treatises of Government. A. Millar, J. and R. Tonson, H. Woodfall, J. Rivington, et al.

Marx, K., & Engels, F. (1848). The Communist Manifesto. London: League of the Just.

Piketty, T. (2014). Capital in the Twenty-First Century. Harvard University Press.

Rawls, J. (1971). A Theory of Justice. Harvard University Press.

Smith, A. (1776). An Inquiry into the Nature and Causes of the Wealth of Nations. London: W. Strahan and T. Cadell.

Epilogue

Reclaiming America: Strategies for Renewal

Amidst the increasing sway of leftist and socialist ideologies, Americans stand at a pivotal juncture that calls for a unified effort to reaffirm the nation's foundational values of liberty, democracy, and prosperity. The purpose of this chapter is to provide a multidimensional plan that aims to counterbalance extreme influences and revitalize America's essential beliefs. The strategy takes inspiration from President Trump's immigration policy and adopts components of Canada's skilled immigration system.

1. Promoting Civic Engagement

The essence of revitalizing America lies in fostering active civic participation. The participation of citizens in the democratic process extends beyond the act of voting; it includes participation in grassroots activity, participation in public debate, and holding officials responsible for their actions. It is the active populace that becomes the driving force in shaping the direction of the nation, ensuring that policies reflect the genuine spirit of American ideals (Putnam, 2000). An engaged citizenry is knowledgeable and vocal about their views.

2. Strengthening Education

At democracy's foundation is a well-educated populace. An educational paradigm that places a priority on critical thinking, civic duty, and a nuanced knowledge of the historical and cultural legacy of the United States of America is required to combat extreme ideas. According to

Westheimer and Kahne (2004), it is essential to make investments in education of a high quality that promotes intellectual inquiry and resistance against disinformation to equip future generations with the ability to resolutely advocate for democratic value systems.

3. Defending Free Speech and Press Freedom

The pillars of free speech and press freedom stand as bulwarks against authoritarianism. Keeping a watchful eye out for these liberties is of the utmost importance in light of the growing number of attempts at censorship and manipulation of the media. According to Mill (1859), society would be able to guarantee the vitality and integrity of its democratic discourse if it supported an unrestricted flow of ideas and fostered an atmosphere that was diverse in terms of the media.

4. Fostering Economic Opportunity

Central to the American ethos is the pursuit of economic prosperity. To revitalize the economy of the nation, policies that encourage development, innovation, and fair opportunity are an absolute necessity. According to Friedman (1962), the process of building an environment that is suitable for entrepreneurship and that rewards diligence involves taking many important actions, including streamlining laws, improving tax structures, and stimulating infrastructural development.

5. Strengthening National Security

America's safety and sovereignty are paramount for preserving its values and interests. According to Clausewitz (1832), it is vital to have a comprehensive national security policy that includes powerful defense systems, border integrity, and sophisticated cybersecurity to protect against foreign threats and ensure domestic peace in a global arena that is continually expanding.

6. Immigration Reform

A coherent immigration policy is vital for sustaining America's greatness. It is possible to improve the nation's economic and cultural fabric by accepting individuals who are prepared to contribute positively to society (Trudeau, 2015). This may be accomplished by imitating President Trump's dedication to secure borders and a merit-based immigration position, which is similar to the system that is in place in Canada.

7. Promoting Unity and Bridging Divides

In an era marked by division, the call for unity and reconciliation is more pressing than ever. The foundation for overcoming ideological divides is the practice of avoiding narratives that are divisive and instead focusing on discussion and mutual acknowledgment. The United States of America is capable of overcoming partisanship and coming together around shared goals if they demonstrate empathy and a spirit of collaboration (Lincoln, 1861).

Conclusion

The endeavor to reclaim America is a collective calling that demands dedication from every sector of society. Citizens of the United States can stem the tide of extremism and pave the path for a successful and inclusive future if they advocate for civic engagement, protect democratic ideals, foster economic prosperity, strengthen national security, adopt smart immigration changes, and foster social unity.

References:

Clausewitz, C. (1832). On War. Princeton University Press.

Friedman, M. (1962). Capitalism and Freedom. University of Chicago Press.

Lincoln, A. (1861). Inaugural Address. Library of Congress.

Mill, J. S. (1859). On Liberty. John W. Parker and Son.

Putnam, R. D. (2000). Bowling Alone: The Collapse and Revival of American Community. Simon & Schuster.

Trudeau, J. (2015). Speech on Immigration. House of Commons of Canada.

Westheimer, J., & Kahne, J. (2004). What Kind of Citizen? The Politics of Education Reform and the Civic Goals of Schools. American Educational Research Journal.

About the Author

Robert Dobbs is a US Army Airborne veteran and public servant with a background in international relations, management consulting, and education. He has a Master's degree in International Relations, an MBA, and a Bachelor of Science in Public Administration. Robert's writing focuses on themes of resilience, leadership, and personal growth. He transitioned into civilian life after completing his military duties and served in local elected office. He also worked as an education and management consultant in the Middle East and Central Asia.

Acknowledgments

As my investigation and advocacy journey comes to a close, I reflect on the many people whose support, insight, and encouragement helped create this work. Crafting "Reigniting the American Dream: A Bold Blueprint for Confronting Leftist Extremism and Revitalizing Democracy" was a journey of intellectual discovery and personal development and connection.

My family deserves my greatest thanks first. Their steadfast support for my idea, even when it seemed impossible, underpinned my endeavor. Your sacrifices were noted by my patient and understanding companion. Your support over late evenings and early mornings kept me going.

I am grateful to my colleagues and peers whose lively conversations and arguments fostered ideas. Your challenges and questions made me dig deeper and write more clearly and purposefully.

The scholarly and academic community that set the groundwork for this endeavor deserves thanks too. My deepest gratitude to the researchers, historians, and professionals whose lengthy research and writings provided the vital facts and theoretical frameworks I drew on.

I am grateful to the many activists, community leaders, and common individuals whose courage and perseverance inspired me. Your commitment to liberty, democracy, and wealth, often in the face of adversity, embodies the American dream.

This book honors those who think ideas may change the future. I hope it reveals our issues and inspires action toward a more cohesive, successful, and democratic society.

Many thanks for sharing this trip.

www.ingramcontent.com/pod-product-compliance
Lightning Source LLC
Chambersburg PA
CBHW070820250726
48662CB00003B/1019